A FAREWELL TO FAMINE

The Society of the
Friendly Sons of St. Patrick
Philadelphia, Pa.

Donates this book in commemoration of the
150th Anniversary of An Gorta Mór (The Great Hunger)
in Ireland 1845-1852
In remembrance of those who suffered and died
and in celebration of those who survived

By the same author:

"Arklow - Last Stronghold of Sail"
(with Liam Charlton)

"The Life of Captain Robert Halpin"

A
FAREWELL
TO
FAMINE

by

Jim Rees

DEE-JAY PUBLICATIONS

First published by
ARKLOW ENTERPRISE CENTRE 1994

This edition published in 1995 by
DEE-JAY PUBLICATIONS
3 Meadows Lane, Arklow,
Co. Wicklow, Ireland

ISBN 0 9522029 0 5 (case bound edition)
ISBN 0 9519239 1 9 (paper bound edition)

Cover: "American Shipping in the Mersey" by Solomon (1850)

Cover picture reproduced by kind permission of the Board of Trustees of the
National Museum & Galleries on Merseyside (Walker Art Gallery)

Designed and typeset by Printset & Design Ltd, Dublin
Printed in Ireland by Criterion Press Ltd, Dublin

Acknowledgements

During the course of researching this book I have been extremely fortunate in meeting many people from various cultures, backgrounds, and interests. A common thread bound them all. That thread was their admiration for the people whose will to survive and prosper is recorded in this book. Because the story began in Ireland, moved to Britain and finished in the United States, it was necessary to carry out research in these three countries. As always, I found archivists and librarians not only helpful and courteous but also interested in the project and this resulted in co-operation over and above the call of duty. Private individuals, upon hearing the story of Fr Hore and his group of emigrants, also took the project to heart and contributed many hours of unpaid research finding vital pieces of information in the process. I am particularly grateful to Francis Murphy of Hoylake, Merseyside. In Arkansas, Jerry Hendricks saved me months of research. Fate decreed that Jerry and I should meet. At one stage of the research, I was guilty of giving scant attention to the Arkansas connection. By coincidence, at this time, Jerry and his wife Wincie were in Ireland researching the origins of the Hendricks family. Jerry knew that his ancestor, Andrew Hendrick, was one of those who travelled with Fr Hore. He settled in Fort Smith and married Margaret Breen who had made the same voyage, so Jerry had a double interest in the whole episode. While making his enquiries, he was told of my research into the matter and he contacted me. I hope he and Wincie have enjoyed our consequent friendship as much as I have.

Ireland:

In Ireland I am grateful to Ken Hannigan of the National Archives. Ken has pointed me in the right direction many times in the past and he did so again on this project; David Sheehy of the

Dublin Diocesan Archives; Sr Magdalena, Archivist of the Sisters of Mercy; Joe Hayes and the staff of Wicklow County Library; the staffs of the County Libraries of Wexford and Waterford; to Fr John Gahan and Fr Seamus de Val who have done so much to record the history of the diocese of Ferns and who are currently engaged on building a diocesan archive; Fr Vincent, archivist with Mount Melleray Abbey; historians Nicholas Furlong and Liam Charlton; Jennifer Kavanagh who chased down many details; Ron O' Connor whose occupation in a previous existence proved invaluable; Pat Power, Robbie Tyrrell and Dolores Tyrrell for reading the typescript; Billy Lee and Siún Gaffney whose fondness for mice I could never share; to John Tyrrell who also emigrated and Jean who returned home. Not least, Robert Hickson for several reasons.

England:

In Liverpool I was most fortunate in meeting Francis Murphy of Hoylake while researching in the Marine Record Centre. Francis spent more time on covering the Liverpool and shipping end of the story than I could have. I should also like to thank Gordon Read and his staff of the aforementioned Marine Record Centre in the Merseyside Maritime Museum complex. The staff of the Liverpool Central Library in William Brown Street, particularly in the microfilm room, were also most helpful.

United States:

In Arkansas, I am grateful to Russell Baker and staff of the Arkansas History Commission; Sr Catherine Markey, Archivist of Little Rock Diocese, who, despite heavy pressure of work, gave me her time, knowledge and access to material; Sr Eugena Pellin of Mount Saint Mary, Little Rock; the staff of Fort Smith Public Library; the Frontier Researchers for allowing me time to speak to their society and for helping me with further research; Fort Smith Historical Society; Old Fort Smith Museum; the many strands of the Hendricks clan. In Texas - Refugio Public Library; Jackie Barnes of Refugio County Museum for her relentless search through census returns and other State papers. In Missouri - St Louis Public Library. In Iowa - Allamakee Public Library; Allamakee County Records Office; Allamakee County Museum;

Fr Trzil, current parish priest of Wexford; Mrs Gavin; the Mullarkey family; and all those who shared their family histories with me at a parish breakfast on an April Sunday morning. In Louisiana - I am grateful to Fr John Finn, who has done a great deal to record the Irish experience in New Orleans. I am also grateful to the American Irish Historical Society, New York and to James Rodgers, of the Irish American Cultural Institute, St Paul, Minnesota. Without the co-operation of the many descendants in several states - far too numerous to mention - who wrote to me with pieces of family history, the picture would have been much less complete than it is. Thank you all.

Many of the people I met were descendants of those about whom this book is written. Complete strangers - who are now friends - not only gave their time and knowledge to me while I was in America, but they even gave over their homes to me. In this instance, I am particularly grateful to Liz Hendricks of Fort Smith (who had to suffer the consequences of her parents having made the mistake of getting in touch with me when they were in Ireland), Prissy also deserves to be acknowledged; Bitsy and John Cates, Little Rock, not only made me feel at home but also helped me carry out my research; Maxine and Allen Reilly of Refugio, Texas gave me the run of their domain. Maxine, in her work with the Refugio County Museum, was indispensible; and Dan and Jackie Regan of Waukon, Iowa made it possible for me to carry out research in the Wexford area. Dan was with me whether in archives or farmyards. Their hospitality will never be forgotten. As a non-driver, my task would have been impossible without the transport all these people provided. They can now hang up their keys until I return.

Finally, without the wholehearted support of Arklow Enterprise Centre, Wicklow County Council, Wicklow Rural Enterprises through the Leader Programme, An FAS and the Arklow Chamber of Commerce the research and publication of this book would not have been possible. It is part of an on-going project to encourage descendants of Wicklow emigrants to visit their ancestral home.

Principal sponsors:

1. Arklow Enterprise Centre Ltd
2. Blaise Treacy, County Manager, Wicklow County Council
3. An FAS, Ireland's National Training Agency
4. Larry O'Neill, Chief Executive, Wicklow Rural Enterprises
5. Arklow Chamber of Commerce

Sponsors of illustrations

1. Allied Irish Banks, Arklow – Dust Jacket/cover
2. Irish Fertiliser Industries, Arklow – Page 75 & Page 78
3. Avondale Chemicals, Rathdrum – Page 74(t) & Page 74(b)
4. Bank of Ireland, Arklow – Page 69 & Page 70
5. Wood Industries (Ireland) Ltd, Arklow – Page 57 & Page 64
6. Woodfab Ltd, Aughrim – Page 80 & Page 97
7. Pitman-Moore Pharmaceuticals, Bray – Page 82 & Page 83

Sources of illustrations

Illustrated London News Picture Library:– 57, 64, 70, 74(t & b), 78, 80, 82
National Museums & Galleries on Merseyside:–
(Walker Art Gallery) Cover/dust jacket; (Merseyside Maritime Museum) 69
J.B. Murray:– 19(t & b), 20, 22
P. Kearns:– 123(t & b), 125
R. Tyrrell:– 40, 55, 98
Trustees of the Rt Hon Olive, Countess Fitzwilliam's Chattels Settlement and Lady Juliet de Chair:– 23
Diocese of Little Rock Archives:– 38, 94, 96
Fort Smith Hist. Soc. Journal:–
Mount Melleray/New Melleray Archives:– 47, 49(t & b), 115(l & r)
Archdiocese of Santa Fe:– 103(b & l)

Our thanks to all the families and individuals who supplied the other illustrations in this book. If any copyright has been inadvertantly infringed the publisher will be glad to discuss the matter with the copyright holder.

Contents

Acknowledgements		5
Lists of Sponsors		8
Prologue		10
Chapter 1:	The Shaping of Thomas Hore	13
Chapter 2:	Coolattin Estate	21
Chapter 3:	Disaster	26
Chapter 4:	Bishop Byrne of Arkansas	37
Chapter 5:	The Melleray Connection	42
Chapter 6:	Farewell to Famine	51
Chapter 7:	Liverpool – the Emigrants' Limbo	60
Chapter 8:	Water, water everywhere	72
Chapter 9:	New Orleans to Little Rock	79
Chapter 10:	Fort Smith	94
Chapter 11:	Plan B	110
Chapter 12:	Conclusion	120
Appendix 1:	The Refugio Connection	127
Appendix 2:	Passengers who travelled on the 'Ticonderoga', 'Loodianah' and the 'Chasca' .	132
Chronology		157
Notes		161
Bibliography		170
List of Subscribers		173

Prologue

For several centuries now Ireland's greatest export has been her people. It is a fact of life which many generations have been born into, have lived with and have died in distant lands as a consequence. It is still going on.

It has been the inspiration behind a vast amount of literature ranging from pathetic doggerel to high literary achievement. Factual accounts of voyages and the search for a new life on the far side of the Atlantic have been preserved and can still move the reader as few fictional stories can. Visual artists have used the theme to catch the tearful leave-taking of loved ones. At times, particularly in recent years, emigration has been looked upon with a degree of optimism, but more often than not, it has been regarded as a curse which the Irish people have had to bear.

But emigration is not a single identifiable phenomenon. It is a word which encompasses many circumstances. It can be a joyous event, it can be a harrowing sentence which must be served, it can be an escape from poverty or persecution. In the Irish mind, it can be even enforced exile.

For all of these reasons Ireland has lost many thousands of her best people to other countries. In his book, "Ireland and the Irish in Maritime History", Dr. John de Courcy Ireland highlights the contributions Irishmen and women made to the maritime histories of other nations and cultures, because of the political and economic restraints which prevailed here. Likewise, our most educated, courageous and high-minded leaders were forced into exile after the Treaty of Limerick at the end of the seventeenth century in what has become romantically known as 'The Flight of the Wild Geese'. That is why Irish surnames figure prominently in the annals of the greatest achievements of America, Australia, France, Spain, Argentina, Canada and many other countries besides.

These early migrations were of people who possessed the natural talents to achieve greater things if allowed the opportunity to do so, whether on the continental mainland or further afield on the far side of the world.

Throughout the eighteenth century and into the opening decades of the nineteenth, the emigrant profile changed slightly. There were fewer political exiles or refugees. The main exception being those who were deported to Australia for subversion or open rebellion against the Crown and, it must be admitted, a fair sprinkling of common criminals. This was a time when the majority of emigrants were optimistic individuals who had the finances to pay their way to what they saw as lands of opportunity, particularly the United States of America and British North America (Canada). They were usually the junior sons of large farmers and were mainly Protestant.

There was a marked difference between the inheritance of property in the Catholic and the Protestant traditions. The Catholics tended to divide whatever land they had (which because of the Penal Laws was usually fairly small in any case) between their sons. The Protestants practised the custom of primo-geniture by which the eldest son inherited the family property. This meant that the younger sons had to make their own way in life, perhaps with a monetary pay-off by way of compensation. It was these younger Protestant sons who were the Irish emigrants of pre-Famine days.

But the 1840s were to change that picture totally and irrevocably. The natural disaster which history has dubbed 'The Great Irish Famine' produced a flood of human misery which poured across the Atlantic. These people did not leave Ireland with money jingling in their pockets or hope in their hearts. They did not sail *to* anywhere, they simply sailed *from* Ireland. There was no optimism, only fear of what might lie ahead. They overcame that fear because of the knowledge of what lay behind.

All they brought with them was the will to survive. Perhaps there was also the faint half-hope that maybe, someday in the new land, their children or grandchildren could live without the fear of regular periods of hunger, and the constant impositions of religious and political repression.

These poverty-stricken and, in many cases, illiterate people, who were turfed out of their homes on the estates of the landed gentry, were despised all the way along the emigration route. Their reception in the new world left a great deal to be desired, but they had survived too much to be driven back to where they came from – besides, few things in the new world were as bad as what they had escaped from in the old. So they stayed and put down roots. Many prospered and, in so doing, repaid their adoptive country many times over. These people did not want anything for nothing. They worked with hard physical labour and with business acumen, whichever was their forte.

Once the threat of hunger was behind them they gained in self-confidence and self-respect. They opened factories, worked the land, studied and taught. They became politically aware and socially active. A few founded dynasties which still thrive in the fields of politics and commerce. The vast majority led normal, decent, hard-working lives. Despite the hardships they had endured in Ireland, they could never forget the country to which they belonged. They passed down stories and songs, perpetuating Ireland's oral tradition. They created images in the minds of their American-born descendants. In many cases these were distorted images fashioned by nostalgia and sometimes tinged with unremitting bitterness. Above all, their love of their native place survived. It is a love that is evident in the Irish-Americans of today, one hundred and fifty years later.

This book follows the fortunes of a large group of people who left south County Wicklow and north County Wexford in 1850. In several respects, these people differed from the hundreds of thousands of other Irish emigrants who stepped off leaky, battered ships onto American and Canadian soil that same year. They were led by a man they trusted and looked up to; they had a little capital with which to build a future; they had somewhere definite to go; but they too were to suffer greatly as their plans met setback after setback.

There are an estimated forty million American citizens who claim Irish descent. There are many more in Canada and Australia. This is what some of their ancestors went through.

CHAPTER 1

The Shaping of Thomas Hore

Fr Thomas Hore is undoubtedly the central figure in the story that follows. Without him the large group who left their homes in Wicklow in 1850 would have had to cross the Atlantic as over a million of their compatriots had done, leaderless and lost. To understand why he took on so great a task, when many men his age were keeping one eye on their retirement, we must know something of his past.

His story begins in the closing decade of the 18th century in a quiet corner of County Wexford. His exact date of birth is unknown but it was either 1795 or the following year. His father, Edmond, lived at the descriptively named townland of Coldblow, Broadway in the parish of Our Lady's Island. The other members of the family were Thomas's mother, Alicia, and his three brothers, at least two of whom were older than he.[1]

The Hore family were of Norman origin, that is, they came to Ireland with or in the wake of the Norman arrival in 1169 which led to the introduction of English rule. Over the next six centuries they had multiplied and fractured so that the name was quite numerous and widespread throughout what was to become County Wexford. The names of townlands give evidence to their long presence in the region, for example, Horesland, Horeswood, Polehore and Horetown. Like many Norman families, the fortunes of the different branches were determined by the political stances they took at various periods in history. For example, in the late Middle Ages Edmund Hore married an Irish girl in contravention of the Statutes of Kilkenny. These laws had been introduced in 1366 to halt the erosion of Norman/English power through marriage with the natives and other social interaction. Edmund's penalty was forfeiture of his ancestral lands. Worse still was the fact that Edmund and his Irish wife were murdered by Edmund's uncle David who had tried unsuccessfully to claim the property.

After the Reformation many Catholic families accepted the new Protestant religion in order to retain inheritance rights. Others kept the Catholic faith and were deprived of their lands as a result. The Hores, in common with most Norman families, were split on which was the best thing to do. Some converted to Protestantism, some didn't. This meant that in succeeding generations, some branches were Catholic and some Protestant. In Ireland, religion and politics have been inextricably tied since the Reformation. Catholics, in most cases, were Nationalist. Protestants looked to Britain as the mother country. The name of Hore can be found on both sides of Ireland's numerous internal conflicts. In the Rebellion of 1641, the lands of William Hore and those of Christopher Hore were confiscated for their part in the Catholic Federation. Most of this property was recovered by members of their families who became Protestants.

There was a claim at the beginning of this century stating that the Hores of Coldblow were the rightful heirs to the ancestral home as they were the senior branch, that is directly descended from an eldest son who had been disinherited for refusing to convert to Protestantism.[2] This claim was refuted by the head of the Protestant Hore family at the time.

Whether they were the disinherited heirs to the family fortunes or not, by the time Thomas Hore was born to Edmond and Alicia in or around 1795, theirs was one of the oldest families in the area and they regarded themselves as undoubtedly Irish. They were Catholic both by birth and, which takes greater faith and courage, by choice.

Ireland in the mid-1790s was awash with political intrigue and suspicion. The centuries-old domination of the country by Britain still sat ill with the majority of the people. Not because of high-brow political ideologies or intellectual niceties, but because of repression of political, social and religious freedom. A century earlier a series of draconian laws was introduced by the Protestant King William of Orange and his Parliament after the overthrow of the Catholic Stuart dynasty. These laws discriminated against Catholics, Presbyterians and non-conformists – in fact, against anyone who was not a member of the Protestant or Established Church (that is, the Official Church of the State).

Among the restrictions placed were: No Catholic could hold any office of State. He could not stand for Parliament or even vote. He could not join the armed forces, practice law, buy land or enter into a lease agreement that exceeded thirty-one years. If he already possessed land, he had to bequeath it among all his children (this led to the disastrous situation of thousands of tiny plots of land all over the country in the next century). If one of his children converted to Protestantism, that convert would inherit the lot. On the other hand, if a Protestant married a Catholic he had to forfeit his lands. The result of this was that by the 1790s – the time of Thomas Hore's birth – less than 5% of the land in Ireland remained in Catholic hands.

While the practice of the Catholic religion was not actually banned under the Penal laws, the new measures were designed to bring it to an end eventually if not immediately. It was hoped to achieve this by banishing all monks, bishops and archbishops from the country. Only parish priests were permitted to continue ministering to the people and they had to be registered with the authorities. With no bishops there could be no ordinations of new, young priests. In time, the existing parish priests would age and die and the Catholic Church would cease to function in the country. That was the theory, but the measures merely served to strengthen the Catholic Church in Ireland to a remarkable degree, a degree which it is only now beginning to lose.

With no political or other representation, the vast majority of the people had no option but to give succour to the Church in which they believed. It became not simply a spiritual body but a temporal unifying force as well. The church needed the people to help it in its darkest hour in Ireland and the people needed something to cling to more than ever. This mutual dependence led to the creation of a bond which few could have foreseen.

By 1730, just thirty years after the introduction of the Penal Laws, the situation was relaxed. The laws were still in force, but the enforcers recognised the impossibility of it all. There was simply no way to bring an end to the influence of the Catholic faith in Ireland. A blind eye was turned. Later, one by one the laws were repealed. By the last quarter of the century Catholics were once again entitled to purchase land; by 1793 those Catholics who owned enough property to qualify were entitled to vote. But the pattern of landownership had been set and was to remain for generations to come.

The political upheavals in America and France also had their effect on Ireland. High-minded young revolutionaries dreamed of an Ireland free from Britain; an Ireland in which all men of goodwill were equal regardless of religion or social standing. In 1791 Theobald Wolfe Tone established the Society of United Irishmen to achieve this end, by armed rebellion if necessary. To advance the cause, he enlisted the help of France and in 1796, soon after Thomas Hore was born, Tone arrived at Bantry Bay with French troops, weapons and ammunition. Only bad luck and unfavourable weather aborted the attempt to land. Over the next two years United Irishmen organisers roamed the country recruiting and liaising between local groups, getting them ready for the coming rebellion.

The British authorities in Dublin Castle, with their intricate network of spies and informers, were kept well informed of the organisation's progress. Nevertheless, they sometimes found it difficult to decide which were the better organised counties, those which were quiet and law-abiding or those which were openly rebellious and antagonistic towards authority. In 1796 the government introduced the Insurrection Act, which allowed it to impose martial law in districts in which it was deemed appropriate. Martial law, by its nature, further eroded the democratic rights of the local population.

When the authorities decided to move against the growing groundswell of discontent and subversive preparations, one of the regions it concentrated on was County Wexford. Towards the end of May 1798, the situation erupted into open rebellion and one of the bloodiest episodes in Ireland's violent history got under way.

Two-year-old Thomas Hore was probably to remember little of the rebellion itself, but he was to live with its consequences as all Irishmen and women had to. One of those consequences was the Act of Union.

Throughout the centuries of English (and eventually British) rule, Ireland had, from time to time, been given restricted self-determination through a Dublin-based assembly. It was never more than a 'local authority' and it could concern itself with internal affairs only. It was ideal from the British point of view in that it took away the tedium of dealing with Irish matters on a daily basis yet still allowed British dominion over her in regard to defence and other matters which might threaten the well-being of Britain. The Irish parliament of the 1780s and '90s, however, had done nothing to defuse the unrest which led to the 1798 Rebellion. In fact, it was openly stated in London that the assembly in Dublin had been the main cause of what was essentially a peasant uprising. It was not surprising then that when the rebellion was quashed, London decided to take direct control once more. It was not a difficult matter to persuade the members of the Irish parliament to vote their assembly out of existence, but it was expensive. To finalise the arrangement, the Act of Union became law on the first day of 1801.

To the majority of the people, it mattered little if they were ruled by an alien government in London or by an equally alien government in Dublin. Except for a few rich landowners, Catholics had no say in the running of their affairs no matter where parliament sat. Life in the region – the baronies of Forth and Bargy – was little altered.

Farming was the principal occupation. Root crops such as potatoes and turnips were cultivated in the small fields. The indigenous population could, if they wished, freeze out strangers because they spoke a dialect peculiar to those baronies. This was Yola which was incomprehensible to outsiders. Yola was a form of Anglo-Norman imported to the region in the twelfth century. It managed to survive the evolution of speech patterns elsewhere so that by the sixteenth century it had become something of an anachronism. Not until the beginning of the eighteenth century did its widespread use begin to decline in Bargy and it was still spoken in Forth as late as 1850. The spread of literacy and greater mobility and social interaction brought the old dialect to its demise.[3]

At nearby Ballyfane crossroads in Carne was a school taught by James Fortune. It was here that Thomas received his early education. Among the subjects taught was Latin.[4] Having completed his basic education, he decided that he was called to the priesthood and he enrolled in St. Kieran's College in Kilkenny.[5] In 1820, at the age of 24 or 25, Thomas completed his theological studies.

By coincidence, that was the year in which the Catholic diocese of Richmond, Virginia was founded. On July 11th, the president of Birchfield College, Dr Patrick Kelly, was appointed bishop of the new See. As he made preparations for departure to take up his new responsibilities, Bishop Kelly gave a great deal of thought to the appointment of an assistant. His attention turned to Thomas Hore. Hore accepted the challenge and travelled to America with him. On their arrival at Richmond, one of the first acts of the new bishop was to ordain Thomas to the priesthood.[6] The challenge, however, was greater than expected. It would appear that the reception they received was less than warm-hearted and Dr Kelly soon felt that it was more than he could cope with. He stayed there only a year and a half before returning home to take up new responsibilities in the less exacting diocese of Waterford and Lismore. No successor was appointed to Richmond for another twelve years.[7]

This put an even greater burden on young Fr Hore, who continued to carry out his duties. In 1825, against great odds, Hore built a small wooden chapel on Fourth Street and the corner of I (now Marshall).[8] Eventually, he too found it too great a strain and after six years his health began to deteriorate, compelling him to return to Ireland.

The bishop of his native diocese of Ferns, Dr Keating, appointed him Administrator of Camolin, which was then a mensal parish, that is, a parish over which the bishop has direct control and there is no parish priest as such. He held that position for thirteen years. Then came the appointment which was to lead to the series of events that was to put Fr Hore into a place of honour in the history of counties Wicklow and Wexford as well as into the annals of Arkansas and Iowa in the United States.

It began with the death of Fr Charles O'Brien in April 1841. He was parish priest of the combined parishes of Killaveny and Annacurra. This was one of the most northerly parishes of the Ferns diocese and was, in fact, over the Wexford border and lay in the neighbouring county of Wicklow. To fill the void left by Fr O'Brien's death, Thomas Hore was assigned to there. He had waited a long time to assume the responsibilities of a parish priest and now that he had achieved it, he set to work immediately.

It was an extensive rural parish, boasting three churches. One of these was in the village of Annacurra, another had been built at Crosspatrick in 1825. The local landlord, Earl Fitzwilliam, had no objection to his tenants having their places of worship on his land

The chapel at Crosspatrick which was built in 1825. This is actually in the townland of Bridgeland.

The chapel at Annacurra, one of three in Fr Hore's parish.

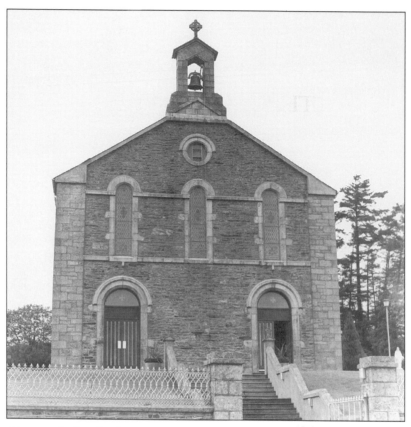

The parish church of St. Kevin's at Killaveny. This was built between 1841-1844, soon after Fr Hore's arrival as parish priest.

and in the case of the Crosspatrick church, he donated £300 and fifteen acres of land so that a house for the curate could be built adjacent to it the year following its construction.[9] Hore would have two curates to help him minister these out-churches, one curate in each district. He himself would be responsible for the entire parish and would be based in the old parish church at Killaveny. In fact it didn't take him long to realise that the parish church was long past its best and one of the first things he would have to do would be to begin work on a new one. It was to take him almost three years to complete, but he saw it through with the determination he had always shown and which he was to show in times to come. On April 20th, 1844, the new church, which was dedicated to St. Kevin, was consecrated by Bishop Keating[10] and the old one was abandoned.

CHAPTER 2

The Coolattin Estate

Hore's parish was part of the Coolattin estate, the owners of which were the Fitzwilliam family. They were among the greatest landowners in County Wicklow during the 19th century. According to Burke's Peerage, the family could trace its origins back to Sir William Fitzwilliam who had lived in England seven hundred years earlier. Throughout centuries of political turmoil their instinct for survival not only saw them through unscathed, but each generation increased the family fortunes. By the 17th century, they had vast estates in England and in 1620 William Fitzwilliam was 'elevated' to the peerage in Ireland, taking the title Baron Fitzwilliam of Liffer (that is Lifford in Co. Donegal). A few generations later yet another William became the 1st Earl Fitzwilliam as their star continued its ascendancy. By this time the family was incredibly wealthy, owning vast tracts of land on both sides of the Irish Sea, and was related to some of the most influential families in both England and Ireland. The Irish estate comprised much of south Wicklow, taking in the barony of Shillelagh, quite a bit of the neighbouring barony of Ballinacor South, and also stretched across county boundaries into Kildare and Wexford. Towards the end of the 19th century, the encumbant Earl added the towns of Rathdrum and Wicklow, the county capital, to his demense. In all, it amounted to about 90,000 acres.

In 1795 the 4th Earl was appointed Lord Lieutenant of Ireland.[1] It was a prestigious post but suited only to someone who did not wish to rock the boat. Fitzwilliam's appointment came just as preparations for the series of United Irishman insurrections, which were to take place three years later, were well under way.

In this exalted position, Fitzwilliam displayed a degree of fair-mindedness which brought him into serious confrontation with his peers. His attack on the lethargy and corruption of the Dublin assembly and its administrators was deemed barely less than traitorous in the unsettled political climate which then prevailed. As a result he was removed from office after only three months.[2] His support for Catholic emancipation also made him 'suspect' in their eyes. He blamed the discriminatory laws for the unrest around the country. To him, religious bigotry was both politically unwise and morally unjustifiable.

In 1796 he built a new country seat at Coolattin near the village of Shillelagh. When rebellion broke out two years later, Fitzwilliam's fair-mindedness was forgotten by the insurgents and the house was burned to the ground. This does not seem to have embittered him against his Catholic tenantry and when an uneasy peace was restored he had a replacement house erected. This mansion, which is still standing, was built between 1801 and 1804.[3]

It is a fine two-storeyed house with a five-bay frontage with three-bay break and wide impediment. It is best described as handsome rather than impressive and was not intended as one of the family's more important seats. Still, it was more than adequate and perfectly suited the role of 'the Big House' on the Coolattin estate.

Fitzwilliam continued his policy of treating his tenants with remarkable liberality. At a time when some landlords would not

Coolattin House, the home of the Fitzwilliam family.

Charles, 5th Earl when 16 years old in 1802.

allow Catholic churches on their estates, Fitzwilliam encouraged his tenants to practice their faith. As previously mentioned, in 1826 he gave £300 and fifteen acres of land to one of the parishes on the demesne so that a house for the curate could be erected.[4]

When he died in 1833, he was succeeded by his son Charles. Charles was forty-seven and he not only inherited the title but also his father's enlightened attitude towards his tenants. He continued supporting schools on the estate. Some were wholly maintained by him, as they had been by his father, others were partly maintained by the Fitzwilliam coffers. One of these schools was in the village of Shillelagh and it catered for 220 boys and girls of all religious persuasions.[5] Charles was the encumbant Earl when Fr Hore arrived on the scene to take up his duties as pastor on the estate parish of Killaveny and Annacurra.

Despite the generally accepted image of the Fitzwilliams being 'good landlords', they were not universally esteemed. In the week in which Hore took up his duties at Killaveny, the nationalist newspaper, "Freeman's Journal", condemned Fitzwilliam's stance in parliament on measures affecting Irish industry: "... all your lifetime wringing tens of thousands of absentee rents from Ireland every year and yet you refused, no later than yesterday, to put your name to a requisition in favour of reviving Irish manufacture".[6] Fitzwilliam, because of his parliamentary commitments and other responsibilites, could be termed 'an absentee landlord'[7], but perhaps it is fair to say that he did not deserve the connotations that description carried. In his absence the estate was managed by his agent, Robert Chaloner, and correspondence between Fitzwilliam and Fr Hore was, for the most part, conducted through him. From letters extant in the National Library of Ireland, it is evident that Chaloner grew to respect Hore although they did not always see eye to eye.[8]

The Fitzwilliams had been astute businessmen for centuries and as early as the 1830s they were well aware that the estate could not continue to support an ever-increasing number of tenants. Unless the system of land tenure was changed, the estate would become bankrupt – a situation which faced many estates during the 1840s.[9] The small holdings would have to be cleared of their tenants and the acreages amalgamated into economic units. To bring this about Fitzwilliam tenants were taken off the estate, their houses tumbled and the people shipped out of Ireland. When the famine arrived, it became more expedient than ever to export the problem of poverty across the Atlantic. Fitzwilliam employed the services of Graves shipping agency in New Ross, County Wexford[10] and thousands of men, women and children were transported to Canada.

These transportations tend to make Fitzwilliam appear as heartless as any of his peers. His record in dealing with his tenants, however, should not be overlooked. It shows him to have been a man of some compassion and decency. His first duty, as he saw it, was that he was the latest in a long line of 'guardians' of the family fortunes. He was responsible for the passing on of the family inheritance to the succeeding generation. It would have been an impossible task for him to maintain the estate and its tenantry under the system and conditions then in place. Wholesale clearance and re-organisation was the only way the estate could be saved. That was his prime concern. Nevertheless, he could not find it in himself to be indifferent to the plight of the poor.

When it was announced in 1849 that Queen Victoria was to pay a visit to Ireland, Fitzwilliam was one of the few members of the aristocracy to object to it. He refused to have anything to do with what he considered was a sham and wrote to his friend Lord Monteagle that a 'great lie' was to be played out. "....false impressions are going to be made and false conclusions will be drawn .... then false government will ensue ... and I would not have had her go (to Ireland) now unless she went to Killarney workhouse... Galway, Connemara and Castlebar. That would have been my tour for her instead of Cork, (and) Dublin, where she will have nothing but falsehoods, unless she draw the right conclusion by seeing the Cove of Cork without a ship in it".[11] The following year, when it was mooted to abolish the Lord Lieutenancy of Ireland, Fitzwilliam was again to the fore in opposition to such a move.[12] The Lord Lieutenant was the government's direct representative in Ireland. Fitzwilliam believed that it was bad enough having no Dublin-based parliament, but if the Lord Lieutenancy were abolished Ireland's voice would never be heard at all.

He was from a long line of men who spoke out when they felt it necessary, whether their ideas were politically wise or not. In that, he had something in common with Thomas Hore.

CHAPTER 3

Disaster

Few episodes in Irish history have affected the nation so deeply as the failure of the potato crops in the latter half of the 1840s. The consequent famine destroyed the fabric of Irish society, particularly in rural areas. The lack of response by the British government copper-fastened anti-British feeling in a way that was more enduring and deep-seated than mere political differences ever could. It brought about an exodus of Irish people who faced the horrors of a transAtlantic voyage to begin a new life in America and Canada. They went because the alternative was to stay at home and die of starvation or, more likely, from disease. Descendants of these emigrants, nurtured on tales of the 'old country', laced with examples of British apathy and intransigence, were to establish social and political movements that would later support Irish aspirations for independence.

Because of all these factors the famine was probably the greatest watershed in the annals of Ireland. It could and should have been avoided. It was 'inevitable' only in so much as nothing was done to take corrective action decades previously, despite repeated warnings that such action was urgently needed.

Signs that a major catastrophe was waiting to happen had exhibited themselves on a regular basis for many years. It all stemmed from the over-dependence of the poor on the potato as the main – and often the only – diet. This over-dependence had evolved because of the system of landownership prevalent throughout the island.

Soon after the beginning of the 19th century the population of Ireland began to mushroom and the trend continued for the best part of forty years – right up to the eve of the Famine. The reason for this was that couples were marrying younger. Many entered matrimony as early as seventeen for boys and sixteen for girls.[1] One commentator suggested that nineteen out of twenty of these couples produced a child every second year.[2] Such prodigious breeding was bound to have its consequences.

One of the reasons put forward for these early marriages and parenthood was the belief that it was their only hope of security in old age. The children would take care of the parents when they were no longer able to provide for themselves. It must be remembered that this was in pre-welfare days. Even the Poor Law (Ireland) Act was not implemented until 1839. It is now generally accepted that there was also a touch of fatalism on the part of the people with regard to marriage. The level of poverty in Ireland was the worst in Europe. Hundreds of thousands of people lived in hovels that shocked visitors to the country. In such circumstances it was felt that being poor and married was little different to being poor and single. At least being married offered some creature comforts.

Whatever the reasons for the increase in marriages, and resultant increase in population, by 1841 it was estimated that 8,175,124 people were living on the island of Ireland. This had doubled from four million in 1801, a space of only forty years. Benjamin Disraeli believed it to be the most densely populated country in Europe.

How did such a small country feed this population?

As mentioned earlier, under the Penal Laws Catholic property had to be subdivided among all the sons of a farmer when he died – unless one of them became Protestant, in which case he inherited all. After a few generations of subdivision, the average farm of a Catholic family was tiny. On the eve of the Famine, 45% were smaller than five acres. Because of the rents they had to pay the landlord, any cereal crops they grew had to be sold to meet this overhead. Most of the poorer holdings were too small to grow cereal crops either for food or rent. Countless thousands were less than one acre. There is no way of estimating how many of these there were because census workers were instructed not to classify anything of this size as a farm, yet thousands of people depended on such plots for sustenance. Worse still was the plight of the landless labourer, of whom there were also many thousands with families to feed. This most unfortunate class survived through conacre.

Conacre was a system by which a plot of land was contracted out for one crop only. That is, the landless labourer would rent the plot from the owner in order to sow seed potatoes and to harvest them to feed his family. The contract was for that crop only so that there was no on-going lease and the labourer had no rights of tenure.[3] On the other hand, the rent was not payable until the crop was harvested. If, because of blight or for any other reason, there was no crop, the owner of the plot received no rent. It was a gamble on the owner's part for he might receive no payment. To offset this, many landholders came to an agreement with landless labourers by which the labourer worked for use of the plot rather than for a wage. That was a gamble on the labourer's part. All his hope of food and payment for his labour lay in the success of the potato crop. If it failed, his family would go hungry and possibly starve. It was undoubtedly a bad system, but without it, landless families would definitely have starved for they had no other means of growing food and, it must be remembered, to purchase even the most basic foodstuffs was beyond their means.

Ireland was a mosaic of tiny plots of land rented from owners of large estates or sub-let from farmers who had good-sized holdings. There was also a small middle class who owned independent farms. The majority of rural people depended on the produce of the tiny plots for their food and there was only one crop which could yield an adequately high return on such small acreages. That was the potato.

The potato had other advantages as well as being a high yielder. When mixed with buttermilk it provided most of the basic nutrients required for physical health. It was an adequate, if limited, diet. Best of all, because of its high yield and low attention requirement during growth, it was an incredibly cheap foodstuff.

All of these elements made the potato the single most important factor in the Irish economy. If it failed the rural economy failed and the social structure would collapse into disaster. And fail it did, time and time again. Seldom a year went by without some district reporting a blighted crop. Each decade saw at least one widespread failure. Between 1728 and 1844 there were nineteen major crop failures.[4] Most of these took place in the 1820s and

30s. Even when the harvest was good, the summer months were always hungry months as the poor people struggled to survive during the period between the end of one crop and the arrival of the next. Many families had no option but to take to the roads during this annual mini-famine and beg their way to survival.

As the trend towards smaller landholdings increased, so did the people's dependence on the potato increase. As their dependence on the potato increased, so did the devastation caused by a blighted crop.

One government commission after another pointed out the inevitable disaster that was waiting to happen. They repeatedly stated that unless the system of land tenure in Ireland was changed, thereby diminishing the people's reliance on the potato, a catastrophic famine, far worse than those which had caused great suffering in the past, was bound to occur.

Nothing was done.

The summer of 1845 was a particularly fine summer. The crops looked healthy and newspapers reported hopes of a bumper harvest. At the beginning of August the weather broke. Temperatures plummeted and for three weeks the sky was dull and overcast when it was not actually raining. Almost immediately word was received by the British government that a blight was affecting the potato crop on the Isle of Wight off the English south coast. It appeared to be a new strain, similar if not identical to the one which had appeared in North America the previous year.[5]

This was a worrying development. In recent years the English peasant's diet had become increasingly potato based, although not as exclusively as in Ireland. A potato blight in England would have a great effect on the poorer classes – as it had done for decades in Ireland. Within weeks crop failures were reported on the English mainland and in continental Europe. It was only a matter of time before it crossed the Irish Sea. By October it was reported that there was general failure of the crop throughout Ireland. The situation was not hopeless however, and it was felt that if the people husbanded the healthy tubers, particularly the seed potatoes, with the aid of local charities the impact would be minimised.

The state of County Wicklow at this juncture was fairly good by national standards. It had many things in common with the other counties of Ireland, but it also had aspects which were peculiar to it. The most obvious being the fact that the principal landlords, such as Fitzwilliam, were better in their dealings with their tenants than most of their peers. The proximity of Dublin also influenced the aspirations of young Wicklow people in search of employment. In the west and north of the country, there had long been a tradition of seasonal migration to work in the potato harvest of Scotland, "tatty-hoking". In Wicklow there was a marked emigration to Dublin where employment in domestic service and other occupations was to be had. In the 1840s it was estimated that one-seventh of the county's native-born population resided in the national capital.[6]

Nevertheless, despite this outlet for 'surplus' labour and people, Wicklow's population in 1841 was at its highest level. The figure returned in the census that year (126,143) has never been equalled.[7] It was a population that was overwhelmingly rural based, and many of these lived in single-roomed mud hovels which were roofed with the poorest thatch. These were the people who were most susceptible to the annual hungry months between the crops, for like their counterparts throughout the country Wicklow poor, and not so poor, depended on the potato for their well-being.

The first reports of blight in the county reached the authorities in October 1845. Conflicting reports indicated that it was not as widespread as had been feared. Some areas were more affected than others. The Fitzwilliam estate didn't fare too badly, the loss being from one-third to one-fifth of the crop. Although the food shortage wasn't crucial, it was large enough to raise the prices of basic food items and it was the higher cost of food rather than the harvest shortfall which caused the greatest distress among the Wicklow poor.[8] The experience of dealing with repeated famines and the establishment of local relief committees, as well as the introduction of a Poor Law Relief Act in 1839, eased the 1845 distress a great deal. As historian Ken Hannigan has suggested, if the potato famine had lasted just that one year it would not have merited more than a few paragraphs in our nation's history. But it was not a single occurrence. The following year continued and intensified the downward spiral of disaster.

The springtime of 1846 brought new hope and the Fitzwilliam estate found the planting of the potato crop little changed from usual. On average it was down slightly on previous years, but on the whole the level of planting was about 90% that of normal. There was no need to feel that blight waited in the wings. There had been other years when the crop had been destroyed to be followed by good years. Then came the summer and early autumn and the worst fears were realised. The 1846 crop was completely corrupted by blight. County Wicklow, including the Fitzwilliam estate, faced disaster on an unprecedented scale. It marked the beginning of three years of death and utter distress, with the winter of 1846/7 being remembered in common memory as the worst period of all.

The account of one County Wicklow witness of how he first noticed that the blight had struck for the second year in succession typifies reports from all over Ireland:

> "It was a very warm day. I was descending the mountain going towards the seaside about 3 o'clock on that day when I saw a thick white fog gradually creeping up the sides of the hills. When I entered it I was pained with the cold. I at once feared some great disaster. The next morning when I travelled about in discharge of my duty, I found the whole potato crop everywhere blighted. The leaves were blackened and hanging loosely on their stems, and a disagreeable odour filled the air." [9]

Within a month the blight was widespread throughout the county. Several schemes, some reasonable, many hare-brained, were put forward as to how to salvage as much of the crop as possible, but it was to no avail. There was little doubt in anyone's mind the extent of the disaster and the horrific scenes which would greet them throughout the long winter. In many places there wasn't enough food to feed the population past September. There was only one hope and that was the implementation of relief works as quickly as possible. As in the previous year, the food shortage pushed the prices of the available quantities beyond the reach of the poor almost immediately. As the weeks passed, the government instigated relief works and these were quickly inundated by men desperate to earn enough to feed their starving families. But official policy limited the number of schemes in the county and by Christmas there were only 1225 people employed on them – the fewest number per county outside Ulster.[10]

The situation deteriorated so quickly that any means of survival was grabbed at and no thought was given to the future. This was particularly obvious on the land, much of which remained untilled for sowing the next season's crop. Seed potatoes were eaten or sold to pay rent. This was the most terrifying aspect of all. Blight might well strike the crop for a third year in succession, but even if conditions proved the most favourable for years, it would mean nothing if seed potatoes were not planted in anticipation. This short-sightedness, borne out of fear and immediate need to stave off hunger, was to prove unintentionally suicidal.

Under the Poor Law Relief Act of 1839, Ireland was divided into administrative regions called Poor Law Unions. Each Union was responsible for the construction and maintenance of a workhouse where the destitute would be housed and fed at the expense of the more affluent members of the community. Revenue was to be raised by a local tax on property. Its architect, George Nicholls, admitted that its intention was not to address the problem of poverty in Ireland, but merely to keep the Irish poor on the island and not have them emigrating to the slums of English cities as had been the tendency in the 1820s and 30s.

Each Union was managed by a Board of Guardians. The Board was comprised of leading local figures who were answerable to the rate-payers of the district. They were, in many ways, the local authorities of the time and were supervised at national level by Poor Law Commissioners. Their main function, as stated, was the erection and maintenance of a Poor House or Workhouse.

Conditions in these were horrific, even by the standards of the time. They provoked the condemnation of social commentators such as Charles Dickens. Anyone who feels that Dickens used his creative licence to over-dramatise the horrors of the workhouses should read the records of these Boards, most of which are extant. Incidents recorded in the minutes rival the darkest episodes found in fiction. The workhouse was designed to be the most unwelcoming place on earth. This was to keep the number of inmates – and therefore the expense – down to a minimum. Only those who were at death's door contemplated choosing the one which led to the interior of the workhouse. It epitomised the

Despite the appalling conditions which existed in the workhouses, destitute people flocked to them in droves.

lowest ebb in human misery and was to remain a terrifying stigma in the Irish consciousness for generations. Yet despite the dread with which the workhouse was viewed, by the end of that awful year of 1846, the workhouses of County Wicklow were full. Bad as they were, what the poor had to face outside those grim walls was much more terrifying. Those who could still postpone their entering the workhouse crowded to the relief works until the limit was reached and no more men could be taken on.

In September 1846 the Poor Law Commissions circulated a questionnaire throughout Ireland to determine the extent of the crisis. Leading local figures completed the questionnaires for their areas. Fr Hore, in his role of parish priest and member of the local Relief Committee[11], carried out the task in his parish. He could not hazard a guess as to how long the crop in his district would supply the labouring population with food, but he was far from optimistic. They had been solely dependent on the crop for sustenance in previous years. To make matters worse, he believed that:

> "the ordinary sources of employment never gave sufficient work to the labourer in this district, the want of money and the difficulty in procuring food will deter the farmer from

Soup kitchens, some established by government, others run voluntarily, brought some relief to hungry communities

carrying on his usual improvements and very many labourers will be without work except (for whatever) work will be provided for them. Many of the farmers will not have sufficient food for their families in their crops and of course they will not buy to feed labourers". [12]

Hore added that he did not know of any 'extraordinary' work to be commenced in the neighbourhood and that unless the government laid on relief work schemes the people would starve.

One of the principal types of relief work was road construction and repair. On one stretch of road near Tinahely there were five hundred and seventy men working.[13] The district had never known such devastation and deprivation. The workhouses and relief works were not capable of dealing with a catastrophe of such proportions and the government gave permission for soup kitchens to be opened in the more populous areas. There can be little doubt that this measure saved countless lives, particularly as the new year ushered in deteriorating weather conditions. However, had the export of cereal and other crops through Irish ports been stopped and made available to the starving people, and had the government not been more concerned with safe-guarding the sacred cow of the Free Market than with the welfare of the people, the loss of the potato crop would not have been so catastrophic.

The workforces on the roads and other schemes were composed of listless men whose energies were spent on merely surviving. Reports of deaths of people engaged on the schemes or while making their way home from them were common.

By March 1847, it was estimated that more than one-in-twenty people (6,678) in County Wicklow were engaged on relief works. Remarkably, there were reports that many of these had been offered agricultural work to prepare for the new season but they had refused. Why they should do so is unclear, but the government took the reports seriously enough to cut back on relief works. It is not beyond the realms of possibility that the government exaggerated such reports to justify cutbacks which they intended to make in any case. It was about this time that Hore, no doubt frustrated at the bureaucracy which surrounded the half-measures of government, made it known that he wished to resign from the Tinahely Relief Committee.[14]

The withdrawal of relief was immediate, with 20% of schemes closing down. All others were to be closed by May. Only the soup kitchens, some of them government run, others established by charitable organisations, kept body and soul together. To accept the soup was a blow to the pride of many and was to be a comment of derision for a long time to come. Few remarks in Irish usage were as cutting or as heartless as "you (or your people) drank the soup". There was little choice. There is a point when pride degenerates into mindless obstinacy.

That year, infamous in Irish history as Black '47, was the nadir of the famine, but it was not the end of it by any means. In County Wicklow the death toll that year was two-and-a-half times the norm. By national statistics during that horrific period, Wicklow didn't fare too badly, particularly when compared to the counties of the west such as Mayo, but it had wrought irreversible changes nonetheless. Nowhere in Ireland would be the same after it. It would take generations for the scars to heal. It can be argued that they never really have.

Throughout 1848, '49 and '50, the effects of the famine, the population drain through hunger, concomitant diseases and emigration took their toll. Of all three none was to have such repercussions as emigration. It has been estimated that Wicklow lost 22% of its population as a result of the Great Famine.[15]

From 1847 landlords throughout Ireland were clearing their estates of their tenantry. Under the Poor Law Extension Act, landlords were made directly responsible for the well-being of their tenants. They quickly realised that it was cheaper to charter ships and export the problem to Canada. Canada was preferable to the United States because of government subsidies. Ships of all shapes, sizes and conditions left Irish ports. Many of them were sturdy vessels, well capable of crossing the Atlantic, others were less so. Some were so ill-found that they were given the name 'coffin-ships'.

Fitzwilliam had been doing this for years, of course. He simply stepped up operations and between the mid-1840s and the mid-1850s he chartered more ships than before and sent 850 erstwhile tenant families – several thousand men, women and children – to Quebec and other Canadian ports through what has become euphemistically known as 'assisted-passages'.[16] He used Graves shipping agents in New Ross who specialised in the Canadian trade.

Other owners and agents operated in New Ross and Wexford as well. The local newspapers carried advertisements of ships making voyages to Irwin County, Georgia in thirty or forty days. Everywhere was the constant reminder that Ireland, through her people, was haemorrhaging. The 'Independent' ran a serialised account of the experiences of Charles McDonnell, formerly of Wexford, in his new American home. The editor also offered advice to emigrants regarding the rate of monetary exchange and other 'practical hints for the traveller' such as the proper pronunciation of Arkansas.[17]

Thomas Hore agreed that leaving the country was the only sensible course of action, but there had to be a better way to do it. He knew of two. One was with the co-operation of Bishop Andrew Byrne of Little Rock, Arkansas. The other was through the County Waterford monastery of Mount Melleray.

CHAPTER 4

Bishop Byrne of Arkansas

Fr Hore's sense of impotence and frustration was shared by many clergymen throughout the country. For the most part, they were men of compassion. While their primary concern was spiritual, they could not ignore the physical needs of their parishioners. They brought what comfort they could, but there was little they could do to ease the hunger and suffering which surrounded them. There were others, however, who were in a position to offer an escape. Such a man was Andrew Byrne, Catholic bishop of the diocese of Little Rock, Arkansas.

Bishop Byrne had been born in Navan, County Meath, on December 5th, 1802. Like Thomas Hore, he felt he had a vocation for the priesthood and, again like Hore, as soon as his studies were complete he emigrated to America where he was ordained on November 11th, 1827 at Charlestown, South Carolina. Over the next fifteen years he served in various parishes as pastor in eastern states and when the new diocese of Little Rock was established in Arkansas by the Catholic authorities in 1843, Fr Byrne was considered a suitable appointee. On March 10th, 1844 he was consecrated bishop in New York.[1]

He wasted no time in going to his new See, accompanied by two assistants, Frs Corry and O'Donohue.[2] It was a formidable responsibility as his diocese included the entire state of Arkansas and a large part of the Indian Territory which had been assigned to the Cherokee and Choctaw tribes. The state alone covered 53,000 square miles. One commentator estimated that the diocese consisted of 117,048 square miles of unsettled territory, immense forests, mountains, foothills, rivers and lakes. Bears, mountain lions, wild boars added to the dangers of this new appointment.[3]

Bishop Andrew Byrne

Its tiny population was 98% rural and whatever manufacturing industry there was served the farming and hunting communities. It was rough country, where the people had to be equally rough to survive.

At forty-two, Andrew Byrne was young enough to be both energetic and optimistic. Consolidating affairs in Little Rock itself was his first priority, but he was eager to make his presence, or rather the presence of the church he represented, felt throughout the diocese.

He was acutely aware that making an impact was not going to be easy. There was a distinct lack of catechetical knowledge among the nominally Catholic families there and he felt that this was eroding the faith in the region.[4] Also, Arkansas was at last opening up. Settlers were moving in in increasing numbers. A few were Catholic and Bishop Byrne intended to have their spiritual needs attended to. He also wanted more Catholic settlers to join them. Towns were springing up where there had been nothing before. Existing communities were on the brink of burgeoning into cities and, as long as he had responsibility for the diocese, the Catholic Church was going to be part of that transformation.

Apart from Little Rock itself, Bishop Byrne was eager to develop Catholic communities in another town of promise. That was Fort Smith, some 150 miles west of Little Rock on what is now the Arkansas/Oklahoma state line.[5]

Fort Smith was an important frontier post. It was vital in the westward expansion as immigrants continued encroaching on Indian territory. In 1818, a fort was erected at the confluence of the Poteau and Arkansas rivers and was named after Brigadier General Thomas A. Smith. When all was ready, pioneer families ventured to undertake the journey and a community was soon thriving. By 1824, the settlement was so firmly established that the military felt they could leave the civilians to look after themselves while they carried on their policy of pushing still further west to establish Fort Gibson in what we now call Oklahoma. It was in 1836, twelve years after this vote of confidence in Fort Smith's future, that Arkansas became the 25th State of the Union and the federal army returned to establish a small permanent garrison in the old fort.

By the time Bishop Byrne acceded to the bishopric of Little Rock, Fort Smith was a typical frontier town with a mix of houses for the white settlers and wigwams for the Indians. Both houses and teepees clustered around the fort.[6] The bishop felt that the less than impressive assemblage was set to expand with the influx of settlers and he wanted to assess both the reality and the potential. So, in 1844, just months after his appointment as bishop, he set off with Frs Corry and O'Donoghue.

Not surprisingly, he paid a call on the town's only Catholic citizen, a businessman by the name of Michael Manning. Manning was an occulist by profession, but as business in that line was less than brisk in a frontier town, he also ran a mercantile establishment. A staunch Catholic, Manning's house had been used by visiting priests in which to offer mass.

The first Catholic church built in Fort Smith was completed in 1848.

The visit and the meeting must have gone well from the bishop's point of view because he decided that his hunch had been right and that this was one of the places the Catholic Church should have a firm, vibrant presence. He gave Fr Corry the task of building Fort Smith's first Catholic church. Unfortunately, it would appear that Fr Corry wasn't up to the hard life such work entailed. He was not a young man. He had been a Boston merchant and his calling to the priesthood was a late one. Under the circumstances his appointment to so raw a diocese and parish seems unwise. He failed to complete the building of that first church and returned to his home in Albany after only nine months.[7] His place was taken by Fr John Monaghan and he completed the construction of a log church on Mr Manning's property on North Third and Hickory (D) Streets. They called it St Patrick's. It was dedicated by Bishop Byrne on March 5th, 1848. He was assisted in the task by the parish priest, Fr Monaghan, and a Fr Walsh. This landmark in the history of the town and no less in the history of the diocese of Arkansas had cost $258.50, measuring a mere forty feet long by twenty feet wide.[8]

Over the next number of years, Bishop Byrne continued his crusade, but he needed more personnel. They didn't have to be priests, but they did have to be committed Catholics.

Emigration from Ireland had been increasing as landlords cleared their estates of 'unviable' tenants even before the appearance of potato blight. When the disaster struck, the steady flow became a torrent. In Ireland there was nothing but death and degradation; in America, the promise of a future. Bishop Byrne was adamant that the needs of one (the fledgling Church in America) could be the salvation of the other. In 1849 he began recruiting helpers in his task to get Irish people into his diocese.[9] It would appear that one of these helpers was Fr Thomas Hore of Killaveny.[10] As soon as it looked as if his plans for attracting an influx of Catholics were working, he set about arranging to meet their spiritual needs. What he needed was a congregation of nuns who would support the efforts of his over-stretched priests. And over-stretched they were. Round trips of 500 miles to out-lying parishioners in the remotest corners of the diocese were not unusual and the work took a terrible toll on the young men who were driven by their missionary zeal.[11]

In 1850 he contacted the Sisters of Mercy convent of St. Mary's in Pittsburgh, Pennsylvania in the hope of enticing some of the Sisters to join him, but the numbers in St. Mary's were hardly adequate for the work to be carried on there let alone release a group for missionary work in Arkansas. Undaunted, he made a similar request to the Sisters of Mercy in New York, but this met with the same response.[12] He then turned his attention to Ireland for nuns as well as laity.

CHAPTER 5

The Melleray Connection

Near the quiet County Waterford village of Cappoquin is one of the most celebrated monasteries in Ireland. It is owned and run by the Cistercian Order and was there in the time of the famine. It, too, figures in our story. Although it was not established until 1832, the origins of the monastery lie in France and the Reign of Terror which followed the revolution there forty years earlier.

The general persecution of religious houses which accompanied the overthrow of the monarchy and aristocracy brought about an exodus of clerical personnel. Among them was a group of Cistercians who were intent on escaping to Canada via England. They crossed the Channel without too much difficulty, only to find that the ship which was to take them across the Atlantic was delayed. It was as if fate had decreed that they should settle in England rather than going all the way to the Americas. While they were delayed, they met a Dorset gentleman by the name of Thomas Weld who offered them Lulworth Castle with a tract of land to establish a community there. This act of kindness stemmed from a general sympathy which prevaded England for anyone who had fallen victim to the barbarity then sweeping France.

For some time, the monks lived in harmony with their new home, their surroundings and their neighbours. The local population was overwhelmingly Protestant but this didn't mar the relationship of mutual respect which existed between them. The only cause of concern was that because of the different religion of the indigenous people, applicants to join the community were few and far between with the result that there were no new recruits to take the places of those who died. If the trend continued the community would simply become extinct. Whether by chance or by active recruiting measures, applications to join the community began just when the situation looked its bleakest. The majority of these applicants came from Irish communities in England, emigrants who found that life in the outside world did not suit them. There were even some men who came directly from Ireland to join the monks at Lulworth Castle, now called the Abbey of the Holy Trinity.

It was some time after this that rumours began to spread about the community and the goodwill which had hitherto existed evaporated into serious confrontation. One account speaks of sudden, inexplicable 'bigotry and intolerance' towards the monks. The cause of this intolerance is not explained. There had to be a reason, no matter how misunderstood or warped. Investigations into the community were made, but the Prime Minister, Lord Sidmouth, declared the monks 'innocent of all charges' and allowed them to remain in England. Again, just what these charges were is not detailed. There was a proviso to their remaining in England. The abbey was not to enrol any more British subjects – that, of course, included men of Irish birth. This left the abbot with the same problem as before. Had it not been for the Irish, the community would have died out. If Irishmen were prohibited from joining the abbey, it could not remain open indefinitely. There was no option but to seek a new home.

The situation in France had changed in the twenty-four years the community had been in England and religious houses were again free from persecution. Just as they were contemplating moving, the ancient abbey of Melleray in Brittany was advertised for sale.

This was indeed fortuitous, for Melleray was one of the oldest Cistercian abbeys in France. It had been established in the days of Bernard of Clairvaux, the Order's founder, and it was said that he had visited it personally. From that time right up to the revolution it had been in Cistercian hands. To the monks of Lulworth Castle, there could be no better place to start afresh.

They were sceptical of the French government's goodwill and were cautious not to show their hand too early. They asked rich, influential friends to act as intermediaries to negotiate the transaction. When the time came to reveal the identity of the true purchasers, however, the government welcomed them with open arms, even sending a war ship to ferry them across the English Channel.

That was in 1817, and over the next few years the community grew as Italian, French, English and Spanish aspirants applied for membership of the community. But by far the greatest number of applicants were Irish. In fact, the number of Irish applications was greater than all other applications put together.

In 1830, the French authorities were once more hounding religious houses and the abbey of Melleray fell victim to the new persecution. In a reversal of the edict of Lord Sidmouth in England, the French government decreed that all foreign-born monks would have to leave the abbey. As the abbey consisted mostly of foreign-born monks, it was in effect an order to close the abbey. Again, there was the question of finding a new home.

One man was sure where their new home should be. He had been advocating a move there for years. Now that a new persecution had begun, he pressed harder than ever to have his suggestion listened to and acted upon. He was the prior of the abbey, Dom Vincent Ryan and he had been trying for years to get the community to open a house in Ireland. As prior, he was second in command to the abbot and had to accept his superior's repeated refusal to listen. Now the need to investigate new possibilities proved an ally and he was allowed to visit Ireland to find a suitable location for a new abbey.

Ryan spent months searching until he was physically and emotionally exhausted. At last, he acquired a small farmhouse and holding which, although far from ideal, was sufficient to meet the community's needs in the short term. That was at Rathmore, Co Kerry. In June 1831, Prior Ryan aided by a few brothers, set about making the new property suitable for the community.

Meanwhile, the situation in France continued to deteriorate. In September 1831, soldiers occupied the abbey, ordering the monks to vacate immediately. They refused to leave and the soldiers were quartered there with the sole purpose of making life for the community as awkward and as unpleasant as possible. New rules were also introduced. The monks were forbidden to wear their religious habits and under no circumstances were they to assemble together even for prayers in the chapel. In October, all French-born monks were ejected from the abbey. The Irish and British born monks still refused to leave. As citizens, they had the protection of the British Consul. The government then accused them of inciting local peasantry to rebel and cited incidents to support their accusations. The Consul, obviously worried that there might be some truth in the charges, withdrew his support from the monks, leaving them to their own devices. (As will be seen, these charges were remarkably similar to accusations laid against the abbot in Ireland seventeen years later).

Finally, on November 8th, more government troops arrived outside the abbey. When they entered they gathered all the monks they could find, searching every nook and cranny to make sure that none remained. Then they led them off at bayonet-point towards Nantes, twenty miles distant. Any refreshments partaken along the way were reserved for the soldiery. The monks were allowed nothing and when they reached Nantes that night, they were incarcerated in the barracks of St Jacques. The Consul visited them there and was greatly disturbed by the treatment they had received and he revised his official stance in their regard. He made an official complaint and the strict regime was relaxed slightly. He then told the monks that the government was willing to offer them a choice of action. They could either turn their backs on the religious life, find a job and stay in France or they could go to Ireland, in which case a navy ship would be put at their disposal. They opted for the latter.

News of the events reached Ireland before they did and Dom Vincent was on the quay at Cobh to welcome them. He was not alone. The quays were thronged with well-wishers. As soon as it was possible, the monks set off on the two-day journey to Rathmore.

They were sixty-three in number and it was soon obvious that Rathmore was disastrously inadequate. Dom Vincent Ryan set off along the roads of Ireland once again in search of somewhere which would promise permanency.

A friend of his, Fr Fogarty, who was curate in Dungarvan, County Waterford, introduced him to Sir Richard Keane, a wealthy landowner in the county. He offered Ryan a small, badly run-down house and a barn on some land near Cappoquin. The land was poor and exposed. It promised nothing but heartache and unrelenting toil. Ryan took it, seeing the fulfilment of a dream where others saw bleakness. He called the healthiest of his monks from Rathmore and work on establishing the new Melleray got under way. There were times when they faced severe hunger and in the winter months there was little to protect them from sharp winds and snow which sought out every gaping crevice. They won the support of the neighbouring towns and villages and soon each parish tried to outdo their neighbours in helping the monks. Voluntary labour gangs arrived on the scene to dig and build, to clear rocks and turn the earth. What should have taken years to achieve was accomplished in months, but there was still a long, long way to go.

The monks, once ensconced, built a structure that measured 120 feet long by 17 feet wide. In it, they fashioned a chapel, a refectory, a dormitory and utility rooms. All were smaller than needed but it was a milestone to be proud of. Years of building and consolidating followed and always they were short of money. Only unexpected generosity – such as the building supplier, Keating of Dungravan, scrapping a bill of £900, and a £100 donation from the Duke of Devonshire – kept them going. In 1835, the half-completed monastery was raised to the rank of abbey. It was another three years before it could be occupied fully.

From then on, the development of the abbey was an everyday affair, overwatched by the irrepressible Ryan. The strain of his life's work took a terrible toll, however, and he died on December 12th, 1845 at the age of 57. At the time of his demise there were eighty monks in the community. His funeral service was an imposing affair with bishops and priests as well as secular notaries in attendance. All were agreed that he was going to be a hard act to follow.

His successor was another man named Ryan. Dom Mary Joseph Ryan was elected abbot five weeks after Dom Vincent's death, but he held the post for only two years before resigning. Why he resigned is unclear, but during his tenure he had acquired valuable additional property for the abbey. It was his successor, Dom Bruno Fitzpatrick, that played a part in our story.

At the time of his election in April 1848 Bruno Fitzpatrick was thirty-six years old. His promotion to the position of abbot came at a time when Ireland was held in the grip of the Famine. All around him people cried for help. They were leaving the country

Dom Bruno Fitzpatrick, Abbot of Mount Melleray 1848-1893

in their thousands, or were begging from people who had little left to give. Some were dying by the roadside. Others, cushioned by relative affluence, were tightening their belts as their businesses fell apart in the general collapse of the economy. Dom Bruno Fitzpatrick was well aware of the situation which prevailed. There were those who accused him of being aware of much more.

The year 1848 saw yet another band of high-minded revolutionaries who believed that Ireland's only hope for peace and plenty lay in separation from Britain. Consitutional agitation for the Repeal of the Act of Union had fallen on deaf ears and, once again, armed rebellion seemed the only answer. The leaders behind this uprising were known as The Young Irelanders.

The Young Ireland 'rebellion' was without doubt the most farcical attempt to establish an independent Ireland imaginable. Its main architect was William Smith O'Brien. He had been a supporter of the constitutional campaign for the Repeal of the Union, but as the effects of the Famine took hold, he believed that immediate action was necessary. Constitutional means were getting nowhere. Other Young Irelanders were Thomas Davis, who died just before the Famine began, and John Mitchel. Mitchel founded a newspaper called 'The United Irishman' in which he advocated open rebellion, urging the people to prepare for the coming insurrection. Not surprisingly, he was arrested and everything was left in the hands of Smith O'Brien.

In Mount Melleray, Brothers Ryan, O'Leary, Woods and Clarke were later to claim that Dom Bruno Fitzpatrick was a supporter of the Young Ireland movement and had even "encouraged the monks, employees and neighbours to join Smith O'Brien's rebellion".[1] They went on to say that some monks actually did prepare for the armed conflict but stipulated that Dom Bruno was away at the time. On his return, however, he "took them under his wing".[2] Nothing was ever proved that Dom Bruno supported the Young Irelanders and he survived the accusations. His accusers left Melleray, saying that they were being victimised because they had tried to expose the seditious activities they claimed were taking place.[3] They sought permission to open a new house in Rathfarnham, Dublin but this was refused.

Another, less serious charge levelled at Dom Bruno came from Fr Cosgrave, another inmate of Mount Melleray. He claimed that Dom Bruno wanted to close Melleray and move everyone to America. Whether this was true or not is uncertain, but Dom Bruno had instigated the establishment of a new house in the United States soon after he became abbot at Mount Melleray. By July 1849, the land had been acquired and work had begun on the new monastery of Our Lady of La Trappe of New Melleray about twelve miles south-west of Dubuque, Iowa. Not surprisingly, Cosgrave, too, felt that he could no longer remain in the monastery and cited victimisation as his reason for leaving.

New Melleray was in the diocese of Dubuque where Fr Terence J Donoghue was vicar-general. In common with other bishops and vicars-general in the various frontier regions, he was anxious that laity as well as clergy should be enticed into the area. In his estimation, based on thirty years in America, the soil and climate of the region around New Melleray was everything Leinster[4] farmers could wish for. At $1.25 an acre it was a bargain and he suggested that an immigrant colony should have £1,000 to buy as much land as they needed. This would have to be done quickly, because there were elements in Iowa and elsewhere who were unsympathetic to the influx of foreigners, especially Irish foreigners.[5] Fr Donoghue was quite sure which kind of people he

New Melleray

wanted in his diocese. "They must be smart for we are a go-ahead people here".[6]

Fr Donoghue's counterpart in the province of Leinster was Fr Maher. He addressed the farmers of the region, urging them to go to Iowa, but emphasised that those most likely to succeed in America were young, skilled farmers who could afford to buy from

Fr. Francis Walsh, Prior at Mount Melleray was sent to Iowa to run the new house near Dubuque

49

forty to eighty acres of land. They should expect to find plenty of hard work and no luxuries. Anyone who wanted to get-rich-quick should look elsewhere. He said: "We shall take all possible care to admit none to our colony except those who have laid aside all foolish, exaggerated expectancies and have formed ... correct ideas as to the duties and laborious life of the emigrant".[7]

According to one researcher, Fr Thomas Hore was aware of this development.[8] If this was the case, he would also have known that in April 1850, Fr Francis Walshe, prior of Mount Melleray, arrived in Iowa as prior to New Melleray and that Iowa would be a good destination for Irish emigrants. The temporal aspects, good virgin land and healthy climate, would be more than matched by the spiritual wealth of having the new monastery within a few days' ride. Once Hore decided that emigration was the proper course of action to take, he was spoiled for choice. In Arkansas, Bishop Byrne would welcome them with open arms. The same would happen in Iowa. In both places the people would have spiritual leadership even if Fr Hore decided that he wanted to return home after the emigrants had been settled in their new lives.

Iowa or Arkansas? It didn't really matter. Before deliberating too long on the possibilities, he had another task on hand – to find out how many of his parishioners would be prepared to leave with him.

CHAPTER 6

Farewell to Famine

Sunday, June 2nd, 1850 was a day of religious observance as all Sundays were in the parish of Killaveny. On this particular Sunday, however, there arrived a congregation such as had never been seen in the small parish church before or since. They came from miles around to hear not so much the service as the sermon, for this was the day that Fr Hore had promised he would address his parishioners on his intentions of taking those who wished to accompany him to America. They used whatever means they had at their disposal to be there on time.

Among those present was David Lynch, a native of Cork.[1] Lynch was a member of the Royal Irish Constabulary, the military-style police force, and it was his job to record the essence of Fr Hore's sermon and to report it to his superiors who would then pass it on to Dublin Castle, the hub of British rule and administration in Ireland. There the sermon would be examined for anything that smacked of sedition. Fr Hore was not to disappoint them. As Lynch's report is the best – probably the only – account we have of that remarkable occasion, it is reproduced here verbatim. It will be noticed that throughout he spelled the name Hoare.[2] Other unusual spellings are as they appear in the original.

> "Tinahely, June 3rd 1850.
> I beg to state that I attended Divine Service on yesterday at the R.C.Chapel at Whitefield.[3] After Service the Rev. Thomas Hoare P.P. addressed a numerous and mixed congregation who had assembled for the purpose of hearing him explain his views for giving up his parish and emigrating to America and the reasons which induced him to leave this country, etc.

Mr. Hoare commenced by saying that he had promised on a previous occasion to explain to his parishioners his views for leaving this country for America as it might seem strange to them that a man of his age and position in the country should think of doing so. -

He then stated his reasons were chiefly these: – That he commenced his mission in America where he remained many years and therefore was more competent to judge the relative interests and prospects of both countrys. – That he done so as he had the permission of his late Bishop and to encourage younger clergymen as well as the laity of this country to follow his example, believing as he did that the clergy were required more there than here and that the mass of the people would benefit their condition by going there, as he (Mr. Hoare) saw no hope of their prospects improving by remaining in this country but the certainty of inevitable ruin should they remain.

He then proceeded to dwell in forceable language on the contrast that existed between America and this country stating that the independence, prosperity and comfort which the American people enjoy while in this country there exists misery, degradation and starvation.

(He) Said that he believed the people had in great measure initiated(?) these evils on themselves thro their Party animosity, bigotry and ill-will which they entertained towards each other, that such had been the curse of Ireland, the evil consequences of which left Ireland and Irishmen as they were – 'the bye-word and scorn of all civilised nations' – that Catholic as well as Protestant were alike to blame for keeping alive those feelings of animosity towards each other. That England always fostered it and by which she was able to make use of either party at her will for her own purposes.

He then said that as this was probably the last time he would address them on this subject he would speak to them freely and went on to say that Ireland had to thank England and English legislation for all the miseries and sufferings which this country had endured and under which it still suffered. That he was no Prophet, but that he could see that at no distant day England would suffer for her misgovernment and ill-treatment of Ireland. That it was a notorious fact that England was at present despised and distrusted by nearly every nation in the world and had not scarcely a friendly power in Europe to assist her in the event of a war which every day threatened her. That her Irish subjects were every day flying from the country in thousands and he believed and trusted that the tide of emigration was only commencing to flow – That the time would come when England would want Irishmen to aid her in her battles but would not have them to get; that the downfall of England was certain at no distant day and that Ireland too would sink with her.

He then dwelt for a long time in describing the climate, soil, etc. of America; the comfort and prosperity of its inhabitants, etc – and mentioned as a mark of the growing prosperity of the former emigrants from this country the vast sums they were daily remitting to their friends at home to enable them to join them, and quoted several cases of individuals with whom he said he was personally acquainted, who in a few years became men of independence and fortune, and who, if they (had) remained in this country would never have been anything better than paupers.

That their lands were free soil, no rent, Tithe or tax to pay – save county..(illegible)... – that there was no such thing as bigotry known there, that there every man might worship his God in the form he liked, without incurring the ill-will of his brother man, as was unfortunately too often the case here where man made God and His Scripture the causes of ill-will and hatred instead of love.

He went on to say that he intended leaving this country about the commencement of September next and that he would that day commence to take down a list of the names of such as were willing to accompany him, as by going with him it would be a great saving to them as he intended to charter a vessel if he found he had as many ready to go as would enable him to do so and that he expected each applicant would be ready to deposit the sum of 10 shillings[4] as a guarantee to him and as a portion of their passage money.

(He) Said his place of destination was the State of Ohio[5] remarking that it was one of the best in the Union for climate, soil, etc. – that he intended to purchase land there himself and hoped to be able to form a colony there of his own people.

Mr. Hoare then concluded by exhorting all such as could accompany him to do so if they valued their own and their families future welfare and as he believed there was not the slightest hopes of doing good by remaining in this country but on the contrary inevitable destitution.

About 2,000 persons were present, many of whom came a distance of seven and ten miles. I understand that about one hundred persons gave down their names with the intention of accompanying Mr. Hoare and it is supposed that from six to seven hundred persons will leave the country with him".

Just how these two thousand people heard of Fr Hore's intentions is unclear, but relatively easy to surmise. The Catholic church is probably the largest network in the world. Even in countries where Catholicism is a minor religion, priests and bishops keep in touch not only with their congregations, but also with each other. In Ireland, where the Catholic church was such an important part of the social fabric in 1850, no better means of broadcasting information could be devised. In the first instance, it is more than likely that news of Fr Hore's proposed exodus was announced from pulpits throughout the south-east. This, aided by word-of-mouth, would have been sufficient to entice such a large congregation to his parish church on June 2nd. He may also have advertised in newspapers and by posters but I could find no evidence of either.

Whichever method was used, it was highly successful and his sermon made an impact on many of them.

Who were these people who wanted to hear what he had to say?

The popular image of famine refugees fleeing Ireland is always of the poverty-stricken, landless labourer who had to choose between the workhouse (which, in most cases, was already full), death by starvation or desease, or to escape these horrors by crossing the Atlantic. But not all emigrants fitted this description and those who followed Hore were better off than many of their countrymen at that time.

The evidence for this is anyone travelling with Hore had to pay £5 for a ticket. By 1850, few landless labourers would have been in a position to raise £5 for the fare. To those in the lowest income

Counties Wicklow and Wexford. The bulk of people enticed by Fr Hore's appeal came from south Wicklow and north Wexford

bracket, this represented half a year's income. Even the ten shillings alluded to in Constable Lynch's report would not have been attainable by the poorest class of emigrant. Secondly, most of the poorest tenants on the Fitzwilliam and adjacent estates were being evicted en masse and the majority of these were given either free or subsidised passage to Canada. In many cases, they were even given some money to help them start a new life in return for surrendering any holding they might have on the estate.[6] Because of these incentives, it is unlikely that anyone who was really destitute would consider trying to raise the money to travel with Fr Hore's group. While it had the advantage of safety in numbers and the spiritual strength of being led by a priest, it was simply beyond the means of many. As well as that, the poorest people would have had no idea where America and Canada were, or their geographical relation to each other. They would not have had enough knowledge on which to base a preference when deciding on a destination. Those who did know something of the geographical and political realities of America and Canada, but who didn't have enough money to travel to the United States directly, could do what thousands of their compatriots did on arrival in Canada – walk south over the border.[7] An interesting fact about the £5 fare was that the usual fares from Liverpool to New York and Boston were only £3-5-0. Hore quite rightly said that it would be cheaper to travel en masse and to charter a ship. This being so, it is rather strange that the fare should be £1-15-0 dearer than the norm instead of cheaper.[8] Later descriptions of the group also indicate that they were not of the stereotype famine emigrant we have come to accept. One English newspaper said that the group brought £16,000 out of the country with them (although it didn't say how it arrived at this figure) and that they were well stocked with agricultural implements to help cultivate the vast, untouched tracts of land that awaited them.[9]

Based on the preponderance of indigenous surnames and a superficial inspection of parish records, it is reasonable to assume that most of those travelling were from the Fitzwilliam estate, but there were others who joined the Fr Hore group out of personal loyalty and family ties. Among these were the Bulgers and Hore's niece, Sally Esmond, all of whom came from his native barony of Forth in County Wexford. Edmond Stafford was a nephew of the priest. Two nephews of the Bulger family, Frank and George Murphy, also travelled.[10] There were also three seminarians who felt called to the mission in Arkansas.[11]

Throughout July and August and into September, Hore's plan began to take shape. While those intending to travel gathered what belongings they required and sold what was not, the priest confirmed arrangements with Bishop Byrne who was to be in Liverpool en route to Ireland at the same time that Hore hoped to be in Liverpool en route to Arkanasas. The response to his sermon surpassed his expectations. By the time he had all the names and deposits in, there were enough people travelling to charter not one

Irish emigrants leaving home – the priest's blessing. The main difference between this well-known scene and the departure of Fr. Hore's group is the fact that he travelled with them.

or two but three ships and arrangements were made with an agent named Michael Tierney who acted on behalf of the Liverpool ship broker John Taylor Crook.[12]

By the beginning of October all was ready. There were four hundred families, numbering about twelve hundred people in all.[13] Travelling together was out of the question. Accommodation arrangements in Liverpool were such that it was decided that they should arrive in the city in contingents of three hundred at a time.[14] The first contingent left their homes in the second week of October. According to the parish registers at Killaveny, Fr Hore officiated at a marriage there on October 12th, the next such ceremony a few days later was celebrated by his successor Fr Doyle.

Emigration, whether brought about by desperation or ambition, is always a sad affair. In the middle of the last century it had a finality which we in the jet-age cannot comprehend. The emigrant was viewed in the same way as someone who was about to die. When the last lingering leave-taking was complete and they vanished around the bend in the road or over the nearest hill that was the end of their physical existence. In time, letters might arrive telling of their exploits in the New World, but these were the same as messages passed through a spiritual medium at a seance. Emigration was for the best. It was a farewell to famine. Everyone knew that, but such knowledge didn't make it any easier.

James and Fanny Breen had to bid farewell to brothers and sisters. Worst of all was the fact that one of their seven children would not be travelling with them. John, who was twenty-one, eighteen-year-old Patrick, thirteen-year-old Mary, William, who was nine, and Margaret aged eleven, were all going together. Their eldest daughter, twenty-five year old Elizabeth, also travelled with them but here name is not recorded on the passenger list. Only Frances, who was in her mid-teens, was remaining in Ireland. She had entered a convent. Whether in jest or in true reproach, James had said that her decision to turn her back on the world would render her useless to him and her mother in their old age.[15] The pain of separation was experienced by all who decided that they had had enough and were determined to create a better future for their children and for themselves.

Getting to Liverpool entailed assembling the group and making their way to the ship that would take them across the Irish Sea on the first leg of their five thousand mile journey. As they were small farmers, most would have had carts pulled by horses or other beasts of burden. Onto these were piled what clothes and tools and food they were taking with them. At intervals, the women and children might rest their feet by snatching short rides along the way. When they reached their point of departure, the time to sell the carts and animals would arrive. There would be no room for them on board ship. Besides, replacements could be bought or built in America. Only essential items which might be difficult to replace in the new territories were brought. The Bulger family, who settled in Iowa, had a plough for many years which tradition says was brought over from Ireland.

So it was when Fr Hore led the first contingent towards Liverpool, heading east to move west. In all probability they left Ireland through the port of Dublin[16] and whether they went as ticket passengers or whether the ship was chartered as the transAtlantic vessels had been, it was probably the first time that any of them, except Fr Hore, had been to sea.

Conditions on board these vessels were appalling. Many of them carried between five hundred and seven hundred passengers when they were equipped for far less than that number. These people had to stay on deck without shelter. Some ships had provision for a canvas awning, but this did little to ease the great discomfort and danger. This lack of concern for passengers was generally condemned as inhuman. Cattle, because of their value to owners, were treated better. They were accommodated in deckhouses. These shelters could be used by passengers only if there were no cattle on board. If both cattle and people were being carried, preference was given to the animals.[17] Not surprisingly, disgraceful accounts of inhumanity appeared in newspapers concerning the plight of emigrants on the Irish Sea. In 1848, the 'Londonderry' left Dublin for Liverpool on December 1st with 206 deck passengers. Weather conditions deteriorated rapidly and storm force winds whipped the sea into a frenzy. The ship tossed and dipped so much that if the storm did not abate several of the passengers would be lost over the side. On the order of the captain, the crew forced the 206 people below deck – into a space measuring eighteen feet long, ten feet wide and seven feet high. By the time they were released from this 'shelter' seventy-two had died of suffocation.[18] It would have been kinder to allow them to remain in the open to suffer the ravages of the storm as the passengers of the 'Britannia' suffered on the same route four months later. In her case, three of the 414 deck passengers died of exposure.[19]

Hore's group, however, seems to have escaped the worst excesses of the elements, if not the generally overcrowded and unsympathetic conditions. Nevertheless, they must have breathed a collective sigh of relief as they entered the Mersey. The first part of the adventure was behind them – much worse lay ahead.

CHAPTER 7

Liverpool – The Emigrants' Limbo

Liverpool was not a pleasant city, but some of its architectural features were extremely fine and gave the impression that it had always been of major importance. Such was not the case. It didn't feature at all in the Domesday Book of 1086 and the only reason King John favoured the village with a charter in 1207 was because the pool from which the village derived its name was a suitable location in which to assemble a fleet for an invasion of Ireland. Despite this royal recognition, the village continued to languish in obscurity until the 17th century.[1]

The port, if it could be called that, had little to offer. Chester, less than twenty miles south, had been the major port of the English north-west for centuries and it would have remained so had its access to the Irish Sea, the river Dee, not silted up making it impassable for shipping. During the 17th century Liverpool businessmen saw that the town's potential as a centre of trade depended on the development of its port facilities. Other factors also helped. The Great Fire of London in 1666, compounded by plague in that city, persuaded many merchants to transfer their operations to other ports. Several decided on Liverpool. The establishment of new manufacturing industries in Liverpool's hinterland, particularly in textiles, was also a major boost. Lightweight cloth, a mixture of wool and linen (the latter was later replaced by cotton) was intended for use in the warmer climates of the colonies. Mining of salt at nearby Northwich also led to exports through Liverpool. Salt, even more than lightweight cloth, was essential in places such as the West Indies and other British dependencies in the tropics and sub-tropics.[2] Throughout the 1700s, Liverpool continued to consolidate its position as the emerging port of the region. By 1750 it was third in importance in England, after London and Bristol. Towards the end of the century its significance continued to grow as it entered the slave trade.

This was the most vile, degrading and inhuman of trades. It was also the most profitable. After the Treaty of Utrecht in 1713, England was the world's leading slave-trading nation.[3] By the 1750s, English ships carried 40,000 men, women and children each year to begin lives of slavery. They were referred to as 'black cargo' and five-sixths of this trade was carried through the port of Liverpool. Between the years 1783 and 1793, 878 ships passed through the port carrying 303,737 slaves.[4] To make profits even greater, a triangular route was devised. Ships sailed south from the port to Africa, laden with manufactured goods which were bartered for slaves. The slaves, packed in the most inhumane conditions, were then brought to the West Indies and North America for sale – many died during the voyage. The empty holds were then filled with tobacco, cotton and sugar for the run back to Liverpool.[5]

Between 1770 and 1845, one dock complex after another was built along the Mersey to accommodate the ever-increasing volume and diversification of imports and exports. The city grew along with the port, each feeding off the other. Fortunes were made without the slightest thought of moral issues. The demise of the slave trade in the opening years of the 19th century was a blow, but Liverpool was so well established that not even this could halt its commercial progress. The Industrial Revolution was well under way and manufactured goods were being produced as never before. Raw materials, machinery and finished goods had to be imported and exported and Liverpool was glad to oblige.

A new form of human transportation was also required. Slavery had been abolished by parliament, but emigration was just beginning to take off. From many countries of Europe, people who felt that they had better prospects in the Americas than at home were willing to pay well to cross the Atlantic. For the most part, they were educated and had enough money to set themselves up in business in the United States. Many were the sons of well-to-do farmers whose eldest brothers would inherit all by primogeniture. But the Irish potato famine was to change the profile of the average emigrant. In the second half of the 1840s emigration became big business and the scale of profits was unprecedented. Once again, Liverpool shipping companies were quick to see – and equally quick to seize – the opportunities. Soon, it had cornered two-thirds of the market.

In 1850, Liverpool with 367,000 inhabitants was England's second most populous city, being surpassed only by London.[6] It boasted some of the finest public buildings in Europe and its commercial centre, with its spacious streets, smacked of vast fortunes made from the various trades which passed through the port. Slavery, of course, had been its biggest benefactor and there were many who still mourned its passing.

The dock system could not fail to impress. For miles along the north bank of the Mersey, high brick walls loomed, barring access to the equally impressive warehouses which stood behind them. The upper parts of masts and rigging stood remote and imperious. The Albert Dock complex was particularly worthy of awe. There was nothing to compare with it anywhere, and well seasoned travellers, including sailors who knew ports of all shapes and sizes the world over, marvelled at the sheer solidity and wealth of the Liverpool docks.

Steam tugs and lighters moved constantly up and down the river. Barges, working ceaselessly along the canal system that took goods into and out of the industrial heartland, transhipped their cargoes as if there were no end to the law of supply and demand. Few ships lay at anchor in the Mersey itself. Only those which were ready to leave on the next tide could be seen standing clear of the docks. All the rest were cossetted in the stone-and-water paddocks which catered for their loads or intended loads. Up to twenty thousand arrivals and departures could be recorded in a year.[7]

But there was another side to Liverpool. Away from all the hustle and bustle, away from the architectural achievements and wide thoroughfares, the underbelly of the city lurked. Putrid side-streets and alleys, narrow and dangerous, were populated by thousands of forgotten paupers. They lived in hovels, in overcrowded rooms, in ramshackle houses that had long ago given of their best and should have been demolished generations earlier. At the time of Fr Hore's arrival, an estimated 27,000 people lived in dank cellars in the immediate environs of the city centre and docklands.[8] Contagion and hunger were rife. Drunkeness and despair hung over these slums with a finality and completeness that crushed all hope. Liquor dens, specialising in the poisonous rot-gut these people consumed to escape reality, were operating every few doors. This was the English urban form of Ireland's rural degradation.

Survival in these conditions was not easy. There was little room for scruples or decency. Many of the inhabitants had been victims of trickery and theft themselves. That was why they were reduced to such circumstances. Others were born into it and knew nothing better. Still others were simply vile characters who would have sunk to the lowest depths of human existence irrespective of circumstance. Here, the law of the jungle ruled. It was the survival of the fittest and the fittest in this context could not be hampered by goodwill or principle. Morality was a luxury that none of these people could afford and it was the weakest who inevitably went to the wall. Naivety was the frailest weakness of all, and no one was more naive than the unsuspecting emigrant.

One local newspaper reported that: "Crimps, dock-runners and sharpers, dishonest lodging house keepers and pilfering hucksters are a numerous class in every seaport. In no place do these rapacious individuals abound to a more alarming extent than in Liverpool".[9] The purpose of the article was to advocate the establishment of a government-run depot in which emigrants could be temporarily housed as they passed through the port, safe from the hands of miscreants. The Dock Committee, the paper stated, was aware of the problems and intended to press parliament on the issue in the next session. In the meantime, it was business as usual.

Tricking, robbing and brutalising the transient mass of refugees was something all classes indulged in profitably. The shipping magnates in their well-appointed offices did it on a grand scale. Confidence tricksters and muggers were less ambitious but equally ruthless. Boarding house keepers, of which there was a wide spectrum, invariably overcharged and employed every tactic to delay the passengers continuing their journeys. Each extra night they could hold onto them was extra accommodation fees, extra revenue for over-priced meals and extra profit from sub-standard drink. They employed runners, otherwise known as crimps and touts but most descriptively referred to as 'man-catchers'. Runners

It was in crowded dock scenes such as this that the crimps and runners flourished.

would be constantly on the look out for victims. New arrivals to the city were easy to spot. Those who were simply passing through to America or Canada were the easiest to identify. They carried luggage that slowed them down and advertised that they were 'innocents abroad'. Even if they knew where they going – perhaps even on the way to a boarding house or shipping agent whose address they had managed to get hold of – they were accosted by one or two of the estimated four hundred runners who operated around the docks.

The runners would seize upon these people, haul them to whichever boarding house or shipping agent they were 'recruiting business' for and pick up a commission. The amount they got from boarding house keepers varied quite a bit, but the shipping agents (who were also known as 'brokers') usually had to give the runners 7.5% commission on each ticket sold. In many instances the brokers would have made the sale in any case as the traveller could have been on his way to that particular office without the 'help' of the crimp. Nevertheless, he could not refuse the runner his commission. If he did, word would soon spread and that brokerage would be boycotted and future business diverted to rival companies.

Some runners supplemented their income by giving 'advice' to emigrants and acting as bureaux de change. They would 'explain' that English and Irish money was not legal tender in America and it would be best to change it before embarking on the voyage. If they sailed without exchanging their cash for dollars they would be left with a useless currency. Not surprisingly, the rate of exchange offered by these enterprising individuals fell short of that of the high street banks and emigrants innocent enough to fall into the trap ended up with a fraction of what they had before. One case cited a man who parted with £40 in return for forty 'Californian pieces' – about one and a quarter pennies. Other runners had no time for charades. They simply grabbed the travellers' luggage, carried it a short distance and then refused to surrender it until they were paid an exorbitant sum for portage.

Even when emigrants were not fending off robbers of one kind or another, they had to contend with abuse and disdain. In general, attitudes towards Irish immigrants had hardened to a very marked degree and it reached a dangerous climax in 1850.

The growing presence of a new, cheap labour force had its effect on the English workers. Employers used the availability of thousands of destitute men to keep wages low. The native work force was, quite understandably, angered by this development. Unfortunately, their anger was misplaced against the Irish immigrants rather than against the policy of employers who exploited the situation. The middle classes, normally the pillars of society, also viewed the swelling numbers of Irish Catholic immigrants with trepidation and this was brought to a head in October, 1850 – at the very time that Fr Hore and his group arrived in the city. This trepidation stemmed from what the newspapers termed 'the Papal Aggression'.

The pope announced that he intended to re-establish a Catholic hierarchy in England. Catholic bishoprics had been abolished centuries earlier and Pius IX felt the time had come to re-instate them. To Protestant Conservatives this was outrageous and the tone of most newspapers was blatantly biased against such 'papal aggression'. The basis of the objection was that the pope was a political as well as a spiritual leader. Catholics, even English Catholics, were duty-bound to obey his word. This was a direct affront to the British monarch and constituted an immediate threat to the stability of law and order in England, particularly in Liverpool with its thousands of Irish Catholics. The papers had already recorded the high level of lawlessness which characterised the Irish slum-dwellers (without elaborating the reasons for this lawlessness). What would this barely-controllable mass be like if they were organised by a resident Catholic hierarchy, acting on the orders of Rome?[10] Even Liverpool City Council felt it necessary to make an official protest against any re-instatement of the Catholic hierarchy. The Prime Minister, Lord John Russell, also strongly voiced his opposition to such a move, while at the same time claiming to support all civil and religious rights of Catholics. Demonstrations in Liverpool and Birkenhead were causes of severe disquiet.

There was also the question of health. Many people in Liverpool were convinced that the emigrants brought disease into the city. Historians now believe that although Irish emigrants were greatly undernourished, they were reasonably healthy and presented no major health risk. Nevertheless, the fear held by the people of Liverpool was a logical one and is more easily understood than the one of religious animosity. Infection and disease were so endemic to the city – whether brought in by Irish emigrants or not – that the first Public Health Officer in Britain was appointed to Liverpool.

This was the city into which Fr Hore led his group of bewildered emigrants, the majority of whom had never seen a large town before quitting their homes. They were, no doubt, disoriented, but at least their accommodation requirements were catered for.

There was one honest boarding house keeper in the city. He was Frederick Sable (another equally scrupulous individual was to set up a well run boarding house the following year, his name was Marshall, which made a grand total of two). Sabel gave reasonable service, but his prices were beyond the means of most Irish emigrants. He charged 1/- a day for a bed and three meals. In the less salubrious houses, a bed only could be had for four pence. Because of this Sable catered mainly for German, Scottish and English travellers. It would appear, however, that Fr Hore had arranged to have his group stay with Sable. The hotel at Moorfield could accommodate only three hundred people at a time, so it was decided that the group of twelve hundred should arrive in contingents of three or four hundred.[11]

Because of his honest dealings, Sable was not liked by the runners or rival boarding house keepers and every effort was constantly used to divert business away from him. Fr Hore's group quickly became the target of the crimp fraternity but the actual details are somewhat vague. The Liverpool Times of October 31st, stated that the group: "...lived in a large store hired for the occasion, and as this was looked upon as inimical to the interests of the lodging house keepers and the passenger crimps in the neighbourhood of the docks, every expedient was resorted to by these parties to annoy the emigrants and, if possible, to mislead them".[12] But the following week there appeared a letter to the editor wishing to correct that report.

"In your newspaper of October 31st there is a paragraph relating to the emigrants taken out by the Rev Mr Hoare(sic) to the Valley of the Mississippi, stating that during the emigrants' stay they lived in a large store, hired for the occasion, and in consequence got every annoyance from the lodging house keepers. I beg to inform you that not one of them lived or lodged in a store. They were all and everyone located in lodging houses, and were fairly and honestly dealt with. The passengers have left a document with a highly respectable party in Liverpool to correct the misstatement".[13] At the end of the letter the editor added that he had seen the document referred to and was glad to learn from it that their reporter had been misinformed: "We believe the bulk of the lodging house keepers who receive emigrants are respectable and humane and that they disapprove of the conduct of those rapacious people who 'take in' strangers,as much as do any person in the community".[14]

One thing we do know for certain about Fr Hore during the Liverpool stage of the journey was that he kept an appointment with Bishop Byrne, who was on his way to Ireland to recruit support for his mission in Arkansas. A document recalling that meeting is kept in the Archives of the Diocese of Ferns, Wexford, Ireland.

"Andrew Byrne by the Grace of God and the appointment of the Apostolic See Bishop of Little Rock.

To whom all these present may come, Health and blessing.

Know ye that we by these presents give to the Very Rev. Thomas Hore, late of the Diocese of Ferns in Ireland, full and ample Jurisdiction to preach, Teach and administer throughout our Diocese all the Sacraments usually administered by a Clergyman of his order.

And we moreover appoint the said Very Rev T. Hore our Vicar-General and to the especial charge of the flock by whom he is accompanied from Ireland until revoked by me.

> Given at Liverpool
> Under our hand & Seal
> this 22nd day of October 1850
> Andrew Byrne, Bishop of Little Rock."[15]

Now it was official. Thomas Hore was the spiritual as well as the temporal leader of this group of twelve hundred people. He had to guide them through a journey that at the outset was becoming a nightmare. If Liverpool was anything to go by, it was going to be a lot worse than he or anyone could have anticipated.

Thankfully, their stay in the city was a short one.[16] As they arrived and departed in contingents, it is impossible to say how many were in the city at any given time, or if the entire twelve hundred were ever together there.

As Fr Hore had hoped, there were enough in his group to warrant chartering a ship rather than purchasing individual tickets through a broker. Ship brokers didn't own ships themselves. They simply sold space on packet ships. These were vessels which operated to a timetable between designated ports. The brokers received commission from the shipping company on each ticket they sold. This was their main source of income, supplemented by every act of fraud and extortion which they could dream up to relieve passengers of as much money as possible. The icing on their particular cake was when a large group travelled together – such as Hore's group – and chartered a ship. Chartered ships didn't belong to the main packet lines. They were simply hired for the voyage and every penny profit was squeezed from them. They were almost always inferior to packet ships and were manned by inferior crews. Also the legal responsibility for the passengers on a chartered voyage was vague. This left legal redress by emigrants, should they feel it necessary, almost impossible to pursue, even if they could

This is a typical Passenger's Contract Ticket issued by John Taylor Crook. It was issued to James Farrell who sailed on the "Princeton" in May 1851. It will be noticed that the fare in this case was £3-5-0 (see Appendix 2).

afford the legal expense. When a broker chartered a ship, he packed it as tightly as the law would allow – and then packed it tighter still. Legal limits existed, but government measures to control the excesses of unscrupulous brokers were never enforced.

It would appear that Hore used two brokers. One was John Taylor Crook. The other was the well known company of Stanley, Gibbs and Bright. For £5 a head, Crook allowed passengers ten cubic feet of luggage room each, a place to cook and three quarts of water daily. The contract ticket went on to promise weekly rations of one pound of flour (in two allocations of a half pound), five pounds of oatmeal, two pounds of rice, half pound of sugar, half pound of molasses and two ounces of tea.[17] The contract ticket had to agree with the provisions of the law but it is unlikely that the passengers enjoyed all that was promised.

What Crook undoubtedly supplied were two ships, the 'Ticonderoga' and the 'Chasca', while Stanley, Gibbs and Bright handled the 'Loodianah'. These vessels were berthed in three different docks, the 'Ticonderoga' and the 'Loodianah' in Prince's and Stanley docks respectively, while the 'Chasca' was in Victoria dock.[18]

Before the emigrants could embark, however, the law required each to undergo a medical examination to prevent those who were too weak to travel from making the voyage, and particularly to prevent anyone suffering from an infectious disease from going on board the ship. It appeared all very reasonable and responsible, but it was a total farce. To begin with, the Medical Officers were paid on headage. The more people who passed through the 'examination huts', the more money they received. They were given £1 for every hundred passengers 'examined'. If an emigrant could stand, he was deemed healthy. There were reports of MOs not even looking at the people as they filed passed, simply barking out questions without waiting for answers before declaring the examinee fit. The emigration officer at Liverpool voiced his frustration at the blatant lack of observance of the law and said that some days up to sixteen emigrant ships left port. Each could

The Government Inspectors' Office – a complete sham

have one thousand passengers on board all of whom had supposedly been medically examined by the three MOs in the port. The MOs usually worked between ten in the morning and three in the afternoon, not four as proclaimed on the notice.[19] Such examinations must have taken an average one and one-eighth seconds.

Amidst this mayhem and corruption, Hore's example was praised by one of the most influential publications of the time. It was, they said, "the only Irish colony that has ever been organised upon system ..... The event is too remarkable in itself and too suggestive of the true policy which the nation has neglected – to be passed over".[20] It also gave a brief description of the group:

> "This new swarm numbers about 400 families, or 1200 persons, almost all of whom are small farmers. They are said to take out with them a sum of upwards of £16,000 and large quantities of agricultural implements. A portion of them are of Saxon blood, from the barony of Forth, County Wexford, descendants of the English who settled in that corner of Ireland as early as the twelfth century. The high rents charged by the landlords in that district having, as it is said, rendered it impossible for these people to meet their engagements without trenching upon the savings of former years, they are determined to leave the country in a body".

The article went on to decry the fact that such industrious people would not only be of great benefit to Arkansas in particular and the United States in general, but that they would be lost to Britain and should the U.S. and Britain be at war at any time in the future, these people and their descendants would fight against and not for Britain. The reference to 'Saxon blood' was no doubt believed necessary just in case readers might think that Irish people could have managed such an organised exodus on their own.

On October 24th, both the 'Ticonderoga' and the 'Loodianah' stood in the Mersey, ready to clear.[21] On board the 'Ticonderoga' were 450 of Fr Hore's parishioners[22] with almost as many on the 'Loodianah'. They sailed within a short time of each other. The 'Chasca', with the remaining three hundred members of the group on board, left dock eight days later and sailed from the Mersey on November 2nd.[23]

CHAPTER 8

"Water, water everywhere . . ."

The three ships which Fr Hore had chartered were run-of-the-mill vessels in the emigration trade. They carried goods east and human beings west. The 'Ticonderoga', the ship on which Hore himself travelled, was the best of the three.

She was a New York registered vessel of 1,089 tons. A big ship for that time, she sailed with a crew of twenty-eight. Her captain was John S. Farran and he had brought her to Liverpool from New York in twenty-one days. This was not a fast voyage, neither was it particularly slow and it would indicate that the 'Ticonderoga' was a ship of average speed. They had left the American port on September 9th – this was almost certainly her last port of call before crossing the Atlantic. Prior to New York, she had sailed from New Orleans. They arrived in Liverpool on September 30th with 1,365 bales of cotton, 7,517 barrels of flour and 9,000 staves. She was 'entered out' (that is, she was finished discharging and ready for a new cargo) on October 7th. The shipping agent handling the cargo was John Taylor Crook – who undertook to provide the ship with emigrants for the westward voyage.

In Stanley dock was the 'Loodianah'. She was registered at St Andrews, New Brunswick. A 915 tonner, she was sailed by a crew of twenty-three under Captain J. Dallimore. The 'Loodianah' arrived in Liverpool from Quebec and New Orleans with a mixed cargo. From the former port she carried 47 pieces of oak, 86 pieces of elm, 75 pieces of red pine, 527 pieces of white pine and 22,467 staves; and from New Orleans came 13 pieces of pine, 88 pieces of walnut, 427 pieces of hickory, 15 pieces of oak, 153 pieces of locust timber, 300 locust treenails and a quantity of shooks. This cargo was the responsibility of the Liverpool agents Stanley Gibbs, Bright and Company. She also finished unloading on October 7th.

The third of the trio was the 'Chasca' which lay in Victoria dock. She, too, was registered in the United States. Boston was her home port but, like the 'Ticonderoga' and the 'Loodianah', she was a regular visitor to New Orleans. Registered at 658 tons, she was operated by a crew of eighteen under the command of Captain G.D.Wise.

She left New Orleans on August 19th and arrived in Liverpool on September 30th, after a voyage of forty-two days. She carried 1,488 bales of cotton, 188 hogsheads (large barrels which may have been used to ship tobacco as well as wine) and 3 teacases, 109 barrels of flour, 34 lbs of pig bristles, 20 c(ases?) of staves. Like the 'Ticonderoga', the 'Chasca' was under charter to J.T.Crook. She was ready for her new 'cargo' on October 10th, three days after her two companions.[1]

Exactly when Fr Hore and his group embarked on these vessels is difficult to say. Their date of departure, however, would have depended on when Fr Hore and Bishop Byrne met in the city. We know that this meeting didn't take place until October 22nd[2].

After embarkation, the first priority was to find a place to stow their gear and to make their allotted space as comfortable and as personal as the cramped conditions allowed. By law, each passenger (a child under the age twelve was classified as a half-passenger) was entitled to twelve square feet of space or, if there were more than fifty passengers on board without the benefit of a ship's surgeon, the space entitlement was increased to fourteen square feet.[3] It is highly unlikely that they would have been given so much room. Legal entitlements and responsibilities had no place in the harsh reality of the emigrant trade. Chartered ships were profitable. The more people the brokers could squeeze on board, the more profit they made. It was a situation against which there was no defence or redress. There simply weren't enough Emigration Officers appointed to ensure that the law was complied with.

The conditions in the steerage accommodation – in which the vast majority of emigrants travelled – were bleak and basic. The bunks were not individual berth spaces, but measured six foot by six foot and were designed to be shared by four people – that is,

Emigrant scene, between decks. The cleanliness of the accommodation would quickly vanish when the ship was at sea.

each occupant was allowed a sleeping space of six feet by eighteen inches, which was only nine square feet instead of the regulation twelve square feet.[4] This wasn't too bad if the four people sharing a bunk were members of one family, but such was not always the case. Reports of strangers of both sexes sharing these berths were

Steerage. "Home" for five to eight weeks depending on the vagaries of the weather and other factors outside the passengers' control.

frequent. They made "decency and comfort impossible".[5] Legislation was passed forbidding such arrangements, but like all legislation dealing with emigration, it didn't really make the transition from the printed word into reality.

Equally embarrassing, particularly for the female passengers, was the lack of sanitation facilities. Some ships had chamber pots for use in the 'tween-decks, but there was no opportunity for privacy. There were 'heads' (toilet closets) on deck, but these were usually filthy and were too few to cater for a ship-load of passengers. In any case, in rough weather passengers were not allowed on deck to use these toilets or for any other reason. The lack of air in steerage compounded these problems. The stench of too many bodies in too small a space with too few facilities soon made itself felt so that the constant pipe-smoking became more a blessing than a curse.

Cooking, too, entailed its share of problems. According to Crook's Contract Tickets, for the £5 fare, each passenger would receive three quarts of water daily and a weekly allotment of food which was itemised in the previous chapter.[6] If they did receive these quantities they were lucky. Not that it mattered to nine-year-old Margaret Breen. She had no intention of eating any of the food on board. According to family lore, one of the crew in charge of the food was black, the first negro that Margaret had ever seen,

When rations were dispensed, it was a far from pleasant experience.

and she was convinced that the colour would somehow rub off on the food.

The horrors of badly run ships were numerous and diverse. Reports made by officials, enquiry boards and individual philanthropists all testify to the trickery and treachery of captains and crews. It was common, even usual, to find short rations issued. The sale of spirits was a captain's perk. Not surprisingly, there was no restraint on the volume of alcohol purchased and consumed during voyages. This inevitably led to drunkenness and rowdy behaviour which, offensive and frightening under normal circumstances, served to heighten the hellish aspect of the weeks in a dark, dank and putrid place.

British ships were far worse than American vessels in every respect. The ships themselves were older, less suited to passenger trade and the captains and crews were, on the whole, more barbaric in their dealings with emigrants. The passengers of the 'Ticonderoga', 'Loodianah' and 'Chasca', therefore, probably fared better than many of their unfortunate compatriots. Those on the 'Ticonderoga' were particularly fortunate in that Fr Hore didn't travel as a passenger, but as a ship's officer.[7] This certainly would have made widespread ill-treatment and chicanery less easy to perpetrate. Also, the passengers of these three ships were united by a bond which most emigrants didn't share with fellow passengers. The Hore passengers were a group, a single entity, bound by a common goal, family ties or personal friendships. They travelled as a unit. They were a community in transit. This bonding would have given them a solidarity which would have eliminated the vulnerability single families and individuals suffered. And such solidarity was needed, even on American ships where short rations, and even the withholding of food altogether, was not unknown.[8] Those who had been forewarned about these practices, and who could afford it, brought extra rations. It is probable that Fr Hore's group came well prepared. But even if they did, getting an opportunity to cook their food would prove difficult. On many ships, cooking facilities were such that no more than ten people could prepare their food at a time. In some cases, members of the crew prepared and served the food, but this system too was restricted by the facilities available and would prove no more efficient.

First impressions of the ships' accommodations must have filled their hearts with despair. How could they face weeks at sea, on a heaving ocean, in such miserable conditions? Only the thoughts of the hopelessness at home kept them going.

Once the meeting between Fr Hore and his new bishop had taken place and his appointment made official, there was nothing to delay the voyage any longer. On October 23rd, both the 'Loodianah' and the 'Ticonderoga' had cleared their respective docks and were in the Mersey. On board the former, was a crew of twenty-six, while the latter had a complement of Captain Farran and twenty-eight officers and men. They both set sail and cleared the Mersey the following day, bound for New Orleans.

The unusual motion of the ships at sea would soon make itself felt. Seasickness, compounded by the lack of sanitation, made conditions on board such vessels horrific. No doubt, there were those who just lay in their six-by-one-and-a-half feet space neither knowing nor caring if they would ever reach their destination. The short wave motion of the Irish Sea eventually gave way to the big rollers of the Atlantic as they rounded the Tuskar Rock and the rhythm changed. There is no specific record of the voyages of any of these ships, but so many others have been documented that the constant presence of despair and sickness never fails to impress the reader. The 'Ticonderoga', the 'Loodianah' and the 'Chasca', which left Liverpool on November 2nd, cannot have been totally free of the sadness and sickness which were characteristic of emigrant ships in general.

Dysentery would soon make its appearance, then cholera or a similar intestinal complaint which acquired the general label of 'ship fever'. The numbers of those who contracted and died from ship fever in those horrific years, in those horrific ships, will never be known. The only fatality on the ships in question was 28-year-old Mary Kelley who was travelling on board the 'Chasca' with her husband (or brother) Peter. The cause of death was not recorded.[9] Despite the death of only one passenger, the appalling conditions would have been sufficient to break the strongest body and snap the strongest will. What is amazing is not that so many died crossing the Atlantic, but that so many survived.

The days dragged into weeks as the ships, the 'Ticonderoga' far ahead of her companions, left the Atlantic ocean and passed the

Dancing between decks – the best way to relieve the tedium of the long voyage.

Florida Keys, moving relentlessly into the Gulf of Mexico. On December 3rd, she finally made New Orleans, forty days out of Liverpool.[10] The 'Loodianah' was still battling her way across. It would be another two and a half weeks before she too slid alongside the wharf and disembarked her human cargo after fifty-seven days at sea. The poor souls in the 'Chasca', already a week behind the other two, would take no less than seventy days to make the journey before arriving in the Mississippi on January 11th, 1851.[11]

The 'Chasca' did not spend all that time at sea. For some reason, Captain Wise put into St Thomas in the Virgin Islands on December 20th.[12] Why the ship should have been so far south is something of a mystery, but the most likely reason is that she was blown off course and, that being the case, there would have been a distinct possibility of food and water running low. Christmas at St Thomas was, no doubt, preferable to Christmas at sea with short rations even if it did mean a delay in getting to New Orleans.

CHAPTER 9

New Orleans to Little Rock

And so they arrived in the land of promise. The harrowing voyage across the Atlantic was now well and truly behind them. It was unlikely that any of them would ever make the return journey to Ireland. Unlikely, but some did.[1] To all intents and purposes this was now their home. They had suffered greatly. They had endured the ravages of the ocean and the uncertainty of what lay in store for them. They had survived, but their journey was far from over. They had made landfall, that was all. A thousand miles of river travel still faced them with only hope to sustain their beliefs that 'something better' awaited. Not everyone wanted to reach the same goal and it wasn't long before the first signs of disintegration of the group began to show.

For several families, there had been enough travelling. To them, New Orleans was as far away from Ireland as some place called Arkansas was, and they were content to settle in the city. On the opposite side of the spectrum was a group who wanted to get even further away than the intended destination. They had heard of a place far out into the west, in the state of Texas. Refugio it was called, and in that remote spot other Wicklow and Wexford people had settled twenty years earlier.[2] It is more than likely that some of Hore's group had intended going there from the start. That a splinter group did separate at this stage intending to reach Refugio is known[3] but there is no record in the Texas town that they ever arrived.[4]

One family had good reason not to quit New Orleans. Their small son got separated from the group soon after arriving in the port and was never heard of again.[5] Perhaps that family, whom I have not been able to identify, did carry on with Fr Hore, or

New Orleans at the time of the group's arrival. In terms of immigrant numbers passing through the port, it was second only to New York.

perhaps they went out to Refugio. I could find no further reference to the disappearance of the child or what his family did, but it is more than likely that they would have stayed, hoping to find him, no matter how futile that hope might prove to be.

The greatest reduction in numbers in the core group which continued on with the priest was the result of his not waiting for the 'Loodianah' or the 'Chasca'.[6]

New Orleans was a city of bustle and excitement. It must have reminded the immigrants of Liverpool, the experience of which had not been pleasant. It was by far the biggest city and largest port in the state of Louisiana. Up to 1849, the year immediately prior to the group's arrival, it had been the state capital, but for a variety of reasons the legislature had been transferred to Baton Rouge about a hundred miles upriver. New Orleans retained so much of the French influence of colonial days that it must have been a place of great curiosity for people who had been used to Irish ways and only Irish ways. But there was also a strong Irish presence in the city. Several of the leading businessmen were Irish born and had been in the city prior to 1830. It was at their request that St Patrick's Church was built in 1833/4. The French and Spanish services in the cathedral were foreign to them, in more ways than one, and the Irish "wanted a church and a God that spoke English".[7]

The arrival in New Orleans of thousands of destitute Irish fleeing the famine in the 1840s was disapproved of by the 'established Irish' in the city. The newcomers were a threat to the respectable image which the earlier immigrants had succeeded in establishing. As a result, the famine emigrants received little help from their affluent compatriots. This left them very vulnerable because, as in Liverpool, the arrival of a large workforce willing to work for less than a dollar-a-day[8] stirred up the antagonism of the indigenous workforce. The famine Irish were far from popular and it is not surprising that by the time Fr Hore and his group arrived, the Irish poor were to be found in large clusters around the city, banding together for protection and support. At that time, one in every five residents of the city was a native of Ireland. With such numbers and such intense self-dependence, the Irish vote rapidly developed into a powerful political tool. The poor Irish backed the

Democrats, the merchants of earlier emigrations supported the Whigs and were often referred to by the poor as "Orangemen".[9]

The port's immense importance came from the fact that it was here that the Mississippi emptied itself into the Gulf of Mexico. The great river ran from almost the Canadian border in the north to the Gulf in the south, a distance of about two thousand miles, dividing the United States in half. The local Obijawa Indians called it the 'Father of Waters'. It was the highway by which early trappers and pioneers made their way north and west. During the first half of the nineteenth century, its importance grew as the volume of traffic grew and all the while the city of New Orleans grew with it. By 1850, when the 'Ticonderoga', the 'Loodianah' and the 'Chasca' discharged their human cargoes on New Orleans' quaysides, the push west was greater than ever before and the port was the crossroads of commercial life. In terms of immigrant arrivals to the United States, it was second only to New York.[10] In terms of commercial trade, it handled twice the tonnage of its eastern rival.

Much of this tonnage did not take to the high seas. Many of the vessels made their owners fortunes from plying their trade on the system of rivers of which the Mississippi was the backbone, ferrying passengers and goods from Europe, South America and the eastern states of the Union to cities and towns hundreds of miles upriver and up the great estuaries leading to the east and west. The docks of New Orleans bristled with tall stacks belching smoke and shrill whistles releasing steam. River boats lined the banks and jockeyed for position in mid-stream. The largest of these were really something to behold. 'Floating Palaces' they were called and most deserved the title. Multi-decked, brightly painted

The levee at New Orleans

white with a variety of trimmings. They were propelled by great paddle wheels. Some had an enormous single wheel at the stern, while the more opulent boasted a pair of side paddles. In 1850, and from thenceforward, the latter type became more popular and began to dominate the river. No wonder the Mississippi steamboats were to claim a place in the popular imagination and become immortalised in literature.[11] By day, they were gigantic floating wedding cakes. At night, their glamour was even greater, all lit up and majestic in their stately progress. Their tiers of lights and indominatable appearance proclaimed self-confidence and mastery over the great Mississippi itself. Palaces indeed. Their interiors were fitted out in like manner. The southern states of the Union in pre-Civil War days had style and the riverboats were undoubtedly part and parcel of that style and ethos.

Even more colourful than the sailing ships and riverboats in this hotch-potch of activity were the people. Mark Twain wrote: "When I find a well-drawn character in fiction or biography, I generally take a warm personal interest in him, for the reason that I have known him before – met him on the river". Every type of person, from cardinal to criminal, from savant to slave-trader,

Going up the Mississippi

sailors, cut-throats, con-men, trappers, missionaries and gamblers, all were to be found in New Orleans and all points north along the Father-of-Waters. The sights, sounds and smells of this sub-tropical port were the antithesis of a small Irish village and the rolling green townlands of counties Wicklow and Wexford, five thousand miles away.

Each evening those steamers travelling upriver would follow a recognised procedure. There is no reason to assume that the day Fr Hore gathered those of his group who were continuing on with him was different from any other. From mid-afternoon tell-tale wisps of smoke appeared from tall funnels. Within a short time, the fires would be burning furiously and the sky would grow thick with great clouds of dense black fumes. Soon, the water in the boilers would begin to turn into steam and the pressure would build just as the excitement and anticipation swelled in the hearts of the passengers. Between the hours of four and five o'clock, the steamers would cast off their lines and manoeuvre out into the mainstream. The paddles, whether on the sides or stern, would turn just enough to allow the vessel to answer the helm. Bows brought round to the north, against the current, shrill blasts from steam whistles, and they were off.

Steaming up the Mississippi had its dangers. While they compared little with the perils of crossing the Atlantic in a sailing ship in November and December gales, they were nonetheless real. The river was wide, but it was also shallow. Mud banks changed constantly, thwarting would-be surveyors and chart-makers. The naval architects who designed the steamboats were well aware of these hazards and one of the characteristics of the vessels was a draught shallow enough to float "on the volume of whiskey consumed on each voyage". Nevertheless, they could – and often did – become stuck and had to be assisted to deeper water before continuing their journey. Such help was always freely given. It was a form of insurance, for the rescuer might well be the next victim. Another danger was the presence of river pirates, but these seldom turned their attention to the larger riverboats.

The perils which Fr Hore and his charges had to look out for most were the tricksters, pickpockets, gamblers and crooks who travelled on board with them.

Slowly they made their way north, passing riverside villages and towns. As they approached the places where they were to pull in to load or discharge passengers and cargo, the pilot announced their impending arrival with a few sharp blasts of the whistle. Ashore, the shout of "Steamboat comin'!" brought all interested parties to the landing stage. Between the towns lay marsh land and flat terrain – 'bottoms' – that showed frequent signs of flooding by the river. Mile after mile up the wide, twisting, treacherous highway they went until they came to the state capital, Baton Rouge. Its importance as the seat of state power and legislature could be sensed from the architecture, but it lacked the zest of New Orleans. Further on they steamed to Simmesport on the west bank and they were still in Louisiana.

Simmesport marked a new stage, however, for while the land on the left was Louisiana, the land to the east became the state of Mississippi. The river now had another role to add to its portfolio, that of boundary, a role it played with other states right up to its source. Travel on the river was slow and it took a couple of days to reach the township of Lake Providence on the Louisiana bank. Just a mere twenty miles beyond this, the state of Louisiana at last ceased and Arkansas, the state on which so much depended, began.

It is easy to imagine the stretched necks and strained eyes of all who had journeyed from Ireland as they stood on tip-toe to get a further few yards of vision once they knew that this was Arkansas. Until now it had been just a name they kept locked away in the recesses of their hearts and minds. Now it was a reality, to be inspected as closely as circumstances would allow, to see if it was anything like they imagined it would be. But it didn't look too different from Louisiana. It wasn't quite so marshy but it was still flat and featureless, unlike the gentle undulating grass-covered lands of what had been 'home'. Surely, there was something special about it? The thought of arriving in this land, the aspirations its name could conjure up had kept them going when their wills had been sapped. Surely, there should have been an aura of some kind? A characteristic that set it apart from anywhere else. When it had been only a name it had been paradise. Now they were here and when night fell no bright star appeared, no pillar of fire acted as a guide to proclaim this The Promised Land. Reality showed it to be of this world and with sighs of resignation the travellers settled back to passing the time and planning what they were going to do. This time their plans were based on fact not fantasy. At least, there was no sign of famine or stench of rotting crops to fill the nostrils. And still the paddles turned.

For another hundred miles the views and details didn't change. Mississippi to starboard, Arkansas to port. Then they came to a point where the river split in two, each branch going either side of a large island. The steamboat took the branch to port and made its way between the island and the Arkansas bank. As they reached the point where the island ended and the branches re-converged, a great outflow of water was seen coming from the west. It was the estuary of the Arkansas River. The Arkansas had travelled almost fifteen hundred miles through Indian Territory, the areas we now call Colorado, Kansas, Oklahoma and right across the full width of the state of Arkansas itself to end here.

To Thomas Hore, it must have been a most welcome sight. It signified the final stage of the great responsibility he had undertaken, for up that river, Fr O'Donohoe awaited them at Little Rock. For the first time since meeting Bishop Byrne in Liverpool a friendly face would greet them with unfeigned and unrestricted friendship. There they would be made welcome. There lay their new homes and new lives. Their journey's end was

The old State Capitol of Arkansas, Little Rock, was one of the few imposing buildings in the city in 1850. It is still standing, but a new, bigger capitol has replaced it as Arkansas's seat of power.

in sight and as they made their slow progress towards Little Rock, the thoughts of their first Christmas in America must have filled many of them with optimism.

As the first signs of Little Rock appeared, the feelings of relief and excitement can only be imagined. Fr Hore would once more set about the task of making sure that everyone was ready to disembark and to stay together. There were some fine wooden houses near the river, mostly painted white, but one building dominated the waterfront and that was the State capitol.[12] As the landing stage neared, he would no doubt have been looking out for Fr O'Donohue, Bishop Byrne's second-in-command. Perplexity soon replaced whatever emotion he felt as it became obvious that Fr O'Donohue was not there to meet them, and after everybody had disembarked and stood anxiously on the landing stage, Hore set out to discover where their temporary homes stood and where they could eat. Perhaps Fr O'Donohue simply had not known about their arrival. Perhaps he had been unavoidably detained. It didn't matter. They were here. That was the important thing. There would be time for handshakes and welcomes in due course. The most immediate necessity was to find the church, their accommodation, make their presence known to the pastor, and settle in.

Fr O'Donoghue had the best excuse of all for not meeting them. He was dead. In his place was a young priest named Fr John 'Pat' O'Reilly who broke the news to the group with the following story.

"While on the mission (travelling the circuit), endeavouring to give the scattered Catholics an opportunity to comply with their duties, he stopped at the cabin in the bush owned by a family named Reilly. Worn and exhausted by hunger, labour and rough travelling, the priest, by persuasion of the good woman of the house, threw himself onto a rough pallet to snatch a little repose while she set about preparing him some food. Mr Reilly, a big, bearded, sunburnt man, was glad to perceive that the reverend guest slept well and long. But when the frugal meal was ready he came to awake him. He found him lying calmly, his hands crossed on his breast, his breviary open beside him, his hat over his face (probably to keep off the devouring insects), his eyes closed – not in sleep but in death.

This family alone formed his funeral cortege the next day, when they laid him with reverent hands in red soil beneath the whispering trees. In after years they removed elsewhere, and today the lonely grave of the apostolic man is forgotten...."[13]

This was a bitter blow to Fr Hore and his group. They had come so far in their flight from death only to be confronted with it as soon as they reached their destination. Hore would have heard so much of Fr O'Donoghue's work from Bishop Byrne that it, no doubt, would have rekindled the memories of his own lonely missionary work in Virginia almost thirty years previously. It would have been impossible for him not to empathise. The fact that he didn't know Fr O'Donoghue personally would have little bearing. They were of one mind, one training, one ambition.

Now, the story takes one of its inexplicable turns. According to most published accounts, Fr O'Donoghue had told no one of Bishop Byrne's plans to bring large groups of Irish people to Little Rock. It would seem that he had intended to begin the work of erecting houses and other preparatory measures on his return from visiting outlying families such as the Reillys in whose home he died of exhaustion. No one knew of Fr Hore's coming. No one knew of the bishop's other immigrant groups. When Fr Hore and an estimated three hundred[14] people arrived in Little Rock, they came as a complete surprise to everyone, including the young Fr O'Reilly. This has been the accepted version of the tale, but ....

On December 20th, 1850 the 'Arkansas Gazette' published the following article under the heading 'Arrival of the Irish Immigrants'.

"Some months ago we noticed that the Rt Rev Dr Byrne, from Arkansas, was then in Ireland, and on his return, contemplated bringing with him a large number of persons from the agricultural districts of that country, and establishing a colony in this State. During the past week, about one hundred of the number arrived in our city, apparently in excellent health. These will be followed in a short time by others, and by the returning spring will number several hundred. As yet, it is uncertain in what portion of the State they will locate, but it is the general impression among them that a suitable place will be found on the banks of the Arkansas west of this city.

As these emigrants have arrived in our midst at a season when the inclemency of the weather forbids immediate operations being commenced and as they are desirous of obtaining employment during the winter months, we hope that the door of hospitality will at once be thrown wide open, and the hand of friendship promptly offer aid and assistance, that thus they may have it in their power to speak in flattering terms of their reception, and induce others of their countrymen who have 'long cried for bread and a stone was given them', to seek in this land of the free a habitation and a home".[15]

Perhaps Fr O'Donoghue didn't let anyone in on the secret, but the newspaper was certainly well aware of it. Irrespective of who expected the group's arrival, nothing had been done to accommodate them.

Many of the group were understandably upset by this. They were tired and dispirited. Perhaps, too, they felt a bit cheated. Worst of all was the fact that several of their number were suffering from ship fever and with their resolve thus weakened, the sickness began to take hold. Some accounts state that a cholera-like epidemic seized the group after their arrival in Arkansas, but it is likely that the privations at home and the rigours of the sea journey and river travel would have combined to sow the seeds of the sickness, even if it was still embryonic enough for the reporter to describe them as being "apparently in excellent health". Whatever its cause, a fever did afflict many of them and it was even more imperative to find food and shelter for the unheralded immigrants. The young priest quickly gave over the parish church, a small brick structure which had been erected on the corner of Louisiana and Seventh Streets in 1844.[16] Despite the "pews making excellent bed frames", a number of the patients died. Twenty is the number quoted by one report.[17]

Those who had enough money to do so decided that it was time to leave Little Rock. They had not travelled so far and endured so much to waste away on a church pew in a land that seemed at first sight to offer nothing more than the land from which they had fled. Arkansas had proved to be not a place of new hope but merely a renewal of old fears. St Louis looked more promising and many families packed their belongings and set off down the Arkansas River once more until they reached the Mississippi. Then they turned north and on to St Louis promising Thomas Hore that they would wait for him there. This further splintering was not at all what he had intended.

Fr Hore was bitterly disappointed, but he could well understand how his people felt. He could not blame them. Those who remained did so because of shortage of money or because members of their families were among the sick. They were stuck in Little Rock and their next thought had to be to find work. Most of them picked up jobs as labourers.

Some accounts suggest that the major disappointment which greeted the immigrants was not death or lack of accommodation, but simply the lack of suitable land. Most of the good land was already occupied and the immigrants had little option but to look elsewhere.[18] Fr Hore is said to have visited several counties in the state looking for property which his group could work profitably before deciding that there was little more he could do there.[19] Whether this was true or not, it is beyond doubt that within a month of reaching Little Rock – and without waiting for Bishop Byrne's return – he too headed east to the Mississippi to rejoin those who awaited him at St Louis.

The editor of the "Arkansas Gazette" followed the story. He recorded the return of Bishop Byrne with more immigrants, accompanied by three professed Sisters of Charity and eight postulants.[20]

The following week an article appeared in the same paper which put the entire episode into an extremely bad light.

"The last 'Banner'[21] hails the recent Irish immigration to this State as an event in the history of Arkansas, to be looked upon with pride and pleasure, and the advent of the ten 'Sisters of Mercy' as an omen of brighter days morally and intellectually for this benighted land. Doubtless the Bishop and his satellites will smile complacently at the Roman Catholic features which the paper wears, and with his broad signet upon it, it will find its way into the Vatican, where his extreme Holiness the Pope may chuckle in his robes at the immense good the 'Right Reverend Bishop of Little Rock' is working for the Church and State. But let us come to the facts. Out of the number of the Irish emigrants who remained after Mr Hore and his crowd fled in dismay and almost despair, seventeen or eighteen sleep quietly beneath the red clods of the Roman Catholic burial ground, a number are now groaning under the torture of disease in various hovels around the city, some convalescents are walking shadows; and few, very few, are able to do a day's labour. When these poor emigrants were crowded into the old Church, withered leaves their bed, ragged garments their covering, and the winter sunlight as it streamed through the shattered windows, the only fire to warm them, death itself entering almost every pew and staring the doomed ones in the face, did the priest here bear medicine to the sick, food to the hungry, and minister it? Did he aught, but shrive the dying and get paid for it? Ask the kind lady who lives in the enclosure, and who was indeed a 'Sister of Mercy', gliding at midnight in their midst, dispensing nourishment and raiment, with no eye to see her but the glazed eye of the sufferer and God's. Ask her how often she went where high mass is said, and entreated for succor and failed to procure it. Ask the miserable tenants of the basement story of the Sprague house, the occupants of the cellar about 'battle row', the wasted inmates of the rooms near the jail, to tell you in their own simple style fraught with native eloquence, their touching story. Ask them if the light of the Bishop's countenance has shone upon them, if any Roman Catholic Sisters of Mercy have ever given them a cup of water, ever spoken a word of common comfort. Nay, ask the rosy in-dwellers of the snug quarters attached to the Church that lifts its cross heavenward, how many hours of sleep they lost at the bedside of the sick, how much food ever went from their board to the platter of the suffering stranger.

But yesterday, you might have seen at nightfall an aged man and woman with their son, one young female and a citizen, leaving the cemetery. They were the only attendants at an 'Irish emigrant's' funeral. No clergyman said: 'Dust to dust, ashes to ashes;' father and son shovelled the cold clay upon the rude coffin, and returned from its melancholy sound, sorrowing to their comfortless abode. The surviving brother told the writer of this, that out of his hard earnings he would have to pay the Church to pray for the rest of the soul of the departed. Can such emigrants benefit any State on earth? This is no crusade against the Roman Catholic religion. We state nothing but facts, and we can call respectable communicants in the Roman Church to the book, who cannot, who will not dare to deny them, and who can add yet more if necessary.

As to the great impetus that is to be given to education in the State by these 'Sisters of Mercy' that is only conjectural. One would judge from the second of the editorials to which we have alluded, that letters had hitherto been entirely neglected in our midst. There are several flourishing female seminaries here, one conducted by an accomplished member of the Church in which the editors of the 'Banner' worship. There is a fine female academy at Fayetteville, one at Washington, and another at Tulip, Dallas county, equal to any institutions anywhere, so that even now parents can find means to educate their children at home, and even now can have guardian for their minds and morals of their daughters, who are in the true and extended sense of the term 'Sisters of Mercy'. These remarks are but just to the various Protestant schools scattered throughout our State.

Both editors of the 'Banner' are absent – we by no means mean to say that no Roman Catholics showed kindness to these unfortunates – one, (Mrs Bingham) in her devotion, sacrificed her life to them; another (Mrs Callahan) is dangerously ill".[22]

As can be seen, the tone of the "Gazette" in regard to the immigrants had changed totally within just two months. In December 1850, it urged the local populace to do all that it could to make the newcomers welcome. In February it felt bound to ask: "Can such emigrants benefit any State on earth?" The scathing attack on Hore, Byrne and the Sisters of Mercy left no holds barred and had it not been for the earlier call to rally around the immigrants, the reader would be forgiven for thinking that the writer of the piece was motivated by nativist bigotry.

It is impossible at this remove to say how much truth lay in the accusations levelled at the nuns and the bishop. The fact that Hore did leave the sick and repair to St Louis after a brief sojourn in Fort Smith is beyond question. Only the interpretation of his actions is debatable. As far as the writer of the piece was concerned it was simply a matter of abandonment of the sick.

Whether Bishop Byrne was motivated by the deplorable state of the remnants of Hore's 'colony' or whether he wished to avoid further bad press, he set about establishing an organisation that would help ease their distress. On St Patrick's Day, March 17th, 1851, he instituted the Little Rock Hibernian Benevolent Society.[23]

CHAPTER 10

Fort Smith

The four weeks which had passed since the 'Ticonderoga' had disgorged her passengers in New Orleans had wrought great changes. Thomas Hore had seen his group disintegrate. There were some on the 'Loodianah', others on the 'Chasca'. A few stayed in New Orleans; still others went west, either by land or across the Gulf of Mexico. The bulk of those who made their way to Little Rock quickly assessed the situation and headed for St Louis.

Patrick Reilly, a seminarian who sailed on the "Ticondroga". He was ordained in Little Rock shortly after his arrival.

The three seminarians, Patrick Martin, Patrick Behan and Patrick Reilly stayed on in Little Rock and were ordained there on the most appropriate day imaginable considering not only their

Irish origins, but also their first names, March 17th, 1851 – St Patrick's Day. Behan was considered "a most eloquent preacher".[1] Reilly, who was thirty-five at the time of his ordination, was appointed Master of Ceremonies at Little Rock cathedral two months later and quickly became very popular in the city. It was a popularity he retained throughout his life. Fr Martin was sent to the south-west of the diocese and in 1853 he received a letter of thanks from the Bishop of Galveston for his work in that part of Texas which bordered the diocese of Little Rock. In that letter, the bishop gave his permission to Martin to carry on his work in any part of the state.[2] Eight families also remained in the Arkansas capital[3] and about the same number informed Fr Hore that they wanted to carry on to the other destination intended for them by Bishop Byrne.[4] Fort Smith was one hundred and fifty miles further west. Hore complied with their wishes and brought them to the frontier town on the edge of Indian Territory, before heading up to St Louis to rejoin those who had fled to there.

Just how they made the journey is uncertain. The river was the most logical route, but some historians in Fort Smith believe the group made their way by wagon train[5] along the road which linked Little Rock with Fort Smith. That would have been a slow, painful process, for the road was bad and was the haunt of highwaymen. Because of the continuing importance of the frontier town, however, pressure had been put on the State government to improve the road link between Little Rock and Fort Smith. On January 17th, 1851 the maintenance of the road became the responsibility of the counties through which it passed. This was to lead to road improvements, but on the day that Hore and his small group headed west from the state capital, travelling by river was still the quickest and safest route. It was in good navigable order and there were boats going to Fort Smith daily.[6] There is certainly evidence that one family, the Breens, went by river for there is a family tradition that when they reached Roseville, about 45 miles east of Fort Smith, the family was offered work. Roseville was at that time the major collection point for cotton for shipment downriver. James Breen needed the money and accepted the offer. It is unlikely that the Breens were the only ones to make the journey by boat.

Fr. Reilly's authorisation.

One of the many new experiences for the travellers was the sight of slaves picking cotton on the plantations.

The region in which Fort Smith stood was once the hunting grounds of the Osages, Quapaw, Shoshone and Comanche Indians. The Cherokee also moved into this area, pushed west when their ancestral lands in Tennessee, Alabama and Georgia were taken over by white settlers. Frequent inter-tribal friction prompted the Federal government to erect a fort at the confluence of the Poteau and Arkansas rivers. This was completed in 1818 and named after Brigadier General Thomas A. Smith.

Over the next four or five years, an increasing civilian aspect entered the military post. Trading with other centres entered a new stage in April 1822 when the the steamboat 'Robert Thompson' reached Fort Smith from Pittsburgh, laden with provisions for the garrison. The following year, the first child of civilian parents was born on the post two days before Christmas. In 1824, the garrison was moved further west to protect white settlers in what we now call Oklahoma. Fort Smith was now a civilian community and the arrival of one or two enterprising individuals guaranteed its steady growth. In 1836 Arkansas became the 25th State of the Union and three years later the military returned and built a new, larger fort, the original one having fallen into disrepair. By 1840, it was felt that the town, which had grown during the absence of the military, should have a proper municipal structure and a mayor was elected. A hotel, a school, and several mercantile establishments added importance and a sense of permanency to the scene. Incorporation as a town followed two years later.[7] But it was still a rough and ready frontier town and many of the houses were of poor quality. One account described it as "a collection of straggling houses of the whites, of wigwams, and of soldiers' barracks on the border line of the Indian Territory".[8]

This was the town Bishop Byrne saw in 1843. His belief in its future was well-founded and, throughout the decade, the population continued to grow. As part of his plans for an Irish colony, he purchased the 16th Section of School Lands at Fort Smith. In all, there were 640 acres from the south-east border of the town to about a mile into the forest.[9] It included the old Fort Belknap, where many of the quarters of the soldiers were still in a habitable condition. The price was $5,250 which Byrne received as a loan from his brother-in-law, Mr O'Callaghan of New York.[10] Not everyone in Fort Smith welcomed this development. This was a time when American Navitism was rife. Nativists believed that

Nativists continually promoted the fear that unlimited immigration would undermine American stability. The two main immigration groups at that time were Irish and German.

98

the United States was already sufficiently populated and that its resources should be reserved for those born in the country – as long as they were white. They wanted no more immigrants arriving and certainly no more Catholic immigrants. Because of their policy of not helping newcomers to settle in, even to the point of not giving helpful information, their movement was also called Know-Nothingism.[11]

Bishop Byrne had purchased the land from John Carnell. Carnell was a commissioner of the school, acting for and on the petition of the local citizens. Other commissioners tried to block the purchase, stating that Carnell had no authority to make such a sale. They were determined to challenge its validity in a court of law, employing Albert Pike one of the state's leading attorneys. Pike's anti-Catholic leanings were well known and it was no surprise that he took such a prominent role in the affair. The case was something of a cause celebre for Nativism and it looked as if they would have no difficulty in getting the decision they sought. On the day of the trial the courtroom was packed. Byrne had decided to play his cards close to his chest. No one knew what technicalities or arguments he intended to use. His legal representative was Judge Hempstead of Little Rock, "one of the ablest lawyers in the State". Hempstead rose to his feet at the appointed time and began to speak. He continued speaking for seven hours. Whether by sound legal argument or by eloquence, he won the case. Perhaps the court was afraid that he might get up to speak again had they not found in his and Byrne's favour. The Know-Nothings appealed the decision, but again Byrne was successful and the purchase was complete.[12]

When Fr Hore and his group of stalwarts arrived, Fort Smith was a bustling town. According to a census taken the previous year it boasted a population of 964 – almost double what it had been ten years earlier. Adding to its air of mercantile activity was the fact that it was the last major supply centre for west-bound travellers – and there were many who intended heading west at that time. The discovery of gold in California in 1849 gripped the nation and for the next few years large groups assembled at frontier towns to begin the long trek towards the Rockies and beyond. Fort Smith was a favourite assembly point, with as many as five hundred people leaving at a time. The streets were crowded with prospectors and potential prospectors, mules and oxen. Prospecting was a gamble. Supplying prospectors was a good, reliable business and the merchants of Fort Smith knew which they preferred.

In all probability, what intrigued the Irish people more than the hustle and bustle of trade were the local Indians.

> "The men wore gay, fringed frocks instead of coats, and red kerchiefs or turbans for hats; but otherwise dressed like whites. The petticoats and frocks of the women displayed as many colours of the rainbow as their purses would permit. Though more civilised than any tribe, the male scorned labor. He trudged empty-handed up from the ferry while behind him was his wife with heavy kegs or other burdens on her shoulders. She was usually followed by a Negro slave who came as interpreter. The Negroes all spoke English while many of their Indian Masters did not".[13]

There were many slaves in Fort Smith at that time. For people from the pasture lands of Wicklow and Wexford, the sight and sounds of Indians and black slaves, Poles, Germans, Frenchmen, and many other nationalities passing through Fort Smith on their way to whatever it was they were seeking, must have been bewildering. With such an array of humanity, it was inevitable that mingled with the vast majority of decent, hard-working, law-abiding citizens were criminals of the worst kind. Murders were common, and at the time of the arrival of our group, two Irishmen had been stabbed to death in different incidents. The immediate proximity of Indian Territory offered a safe haven. It was rugged and vast and outlaws could hide out there indefinitely.[14] The regularity of murders and less serious assaults was decried by the local newspaper.[15]

When the time came for Fr Hore to leave his charges, he did so with mixed feelings. He had known many of them as parishioners and had been a leader to them all since this gruelling journey began. It could not have been easy to say goodbye, even if he was leaving just to look after another contingent waiting for him elsewhere. With this group, at least, his mission was complete. He had promised to take them to Arkansas and he had done so.

It is difficult to identify the families who came with Hore to Fort

This marker stone, which can still be seen in the heart of Fort Smith, was placed in 1858 to define the border between the United States and Indian Territory.

Smith because there were a few Irish families already there. In fact, there seems to have been a strong, if small, Irish community already in place. Between 1848 and 1850 the local paper not only carried a good deal of news from Ireland but frequently announced meetings of the Fort Smith Friends of Ireland. Also, some of the people who had travelled with Hore as far as Arkansas did not follow on to the frontier town until quite some time later. Andrew Hendrick didn't get there until 1853. The Breens, who had stopped off in Roseville, didn't delay too long and they arrived in Fort Smith a very short time after the others. They had a sad tale to tell. Their thirteen-year-old daughter Mary had died in Roseville on January 15th[16] and they buried her there. The body was later exhumed and re-interred in Calvary Cemetery. The family resumed the occupation they had followed in Ireland – farming.

Some of the Irish families who arrived at that time were temporarily accommodated in the old soldiers' quarters. These consisted of twelve large buildings, "mostly of small and short hewn logs, carefully fitted and rendered warm and comfortable with the usual filling-in".[17]

As winter turned to spring, the new arrivals set to work, finding employment and setting up permanent homes. By early summer, they were probably satisfied that they had made the right decision and that the future might fulfil its promise. But then cholera struck, as if to remind them that no matter where they went, death would follow and seek them out. The Arkansas Gazette carried the story under the heading "Cholera at Fort Smith":

> "Since our last (report?) ten persons have died from this disease, viz: On Sunday Mrs Nancy Sabine, Mrs Sanders, Jack Downing, (part Indian); Monday, Capt William Duval, Simon, a negro man of Mr Asa Clark; Tuesday, Mr and Mrs Harrison, Rosana, daughter of Michael Gallagher, aged about eight years; Wednesday, William Pilling, clerk of M E Czarnikow, Mrs Nancy Hill.
>
> We have given above the true state of the case, as it exists in our city, and shall endeavour to make known facts. Rumours in the country are exaggerated ten-fold. The panic amongst our citizens has almost entirely ceased and since the character of the disease has become known, it is easily managed if taken in time! It will no doubt soon disappear".[18]

The last sentence was to prove over-optimistic as two weeks later the same newspaper reported that a further fourteen people had died of cholera and that three more had died the day the newspaper went to press. Michael Gallagher, who had already lost his daughter Rosana the previous week, lost his wife and another child. Mrs J B Lynde lost one child on Thursday, one on Saturday and a third on Sunday. The others were Mrs Birckhead, Mrs Callahan, Patrick Duffy, a child named McKnett, a black child of Col Rutherford's, Maria Palmer, Nancy M'Caslin, Ed Palmer and 'old Mr Gray'.[19]

The small epidemic was short-lived. Nevertheless, it must have been a harrowing time for everyone. But once again they survived and other Irish families joined them from various parts of the United States.

Within a few years, Fort Smith numbered amongst its citizens, McNallys, Breens, Sweeneys, Hendricks, Doyles, Harringtons, Dalys, McNamees, O'Donohoes, Mahonys, Lanigans, Farrells, Daggs, Keatings, Coulters, Scullys, Gallaghers, Connells, Lynches,

William Breen was nine years old when he arrived in Fort Smith. His success in business in later years brought him an officership of the United States Court as Chairman of the Committee on Retail Business.

Decendant of Andrew Hendrick and Margaret Breen, Michael J. Sheehan, was appointed Archbishop of Santa Fe in 1993.

Margaret Breen was eleven when she left Ireland. She later married Andrew Hendrick, another 'Ticonderoga' passenger.

This sequence of photographs shows how one of the 'Ticonderoga' Irish families progressed in Fort Smith.

Dodsons, Luceys, McCaheys, McCarrons, Brogans and Kellys. Some had travelled with Hore, some hadn't, but it didn't matter. They were all Irish, sharing a common experience. They stayed close to each other and depended on each other in good times as well as in bad. They acted as godparents to each other's children, they married among themselves and such marriages were witnessed by brothers, sisters, uncles, aunts.

Andrew Hendrick had stopped off somewhere en route and didn't reach Fort Smith until 1852 or 3. He renewed his friendship with the Breens. They had probably known each other in Ireland and they had been on board the 'Ticonderoga' together. Andrew was now about twenty-three years old. Margaret Breen was fourteen – getting near marrying age in a frontier town. The exact date of their marriage is not known, but it was about 1856 when Margaret was seventeen.[20] Andrew worked on the river, "a boat trucking service to Muskogee" in the Indian Territory.[21] They had twelve children, six girls and six boys. The children, and later the grandchildren, were to remember scenes from their childhood that showed how the emigrants continued an Irish lifestyle. Andrew used to take "the Boston Pilot paper (which) carried news of Ireland. When the paper arrived many of the families met in (the) home of grandfather and grandfather would read the news to them. Following this, the guests related ghost stories and weird happenings. Mother said her sisters and brothers huddled together, too frightened to go to bed".[22]

At some stage, Andrew became a teamster.[23] Some years later, his son, Andrew jnr, went into a business partnership with a man called Dean and they operated a livery stable. As time and technology pushed forward, the livery business became an automobile sales company, but Hendricks and horses have been inseparable and each succeeding generation has included family members who have been horse-owners, traders and breeders. One descendant of Andrew and Margaret is Michael Sheehan. He was born in Wichita in 1939 and entered the priesthood twenty-five years later. In 1993, he was appointed Archbishop of Santa Fe.

The surname Hendrick is now well established in Fort Smith, almost 150 years after the arrival of Andrew in 1853, and there are many branches with surnames of different ethnic origins. One branch, that of Andrew jnr, added the letter 's' and are now Hendricks.

On property once owned by the Hendrick family there is now a spot where Hendricks Boulevard intersects with Wicklow Drive.

Margaret Breen's brother William entered the Fort Smith Rifles, a unit of the Confederate Army, at the outbreak of the war between the states. He was then twenty years old and he was present at the Battle of Oak Hill. He later transferred to the Quartermaster's Department where he remained for the duration of hostilities. When the war ended, he returned to Fort Smith and entered business, eventually becoming the most prominent cotton-buyer in the city. He was to lose almost all he had when a business venture didn't pay off, but he re-entered the commercial life of the city, this time dealing in hardware, and at the time of his death in 1905 he had recouped his losses.[24] Elizabeth Breen, whose name was omitted from the passenger list, remained unmarried and died in Fort Smith in 1862.

William and Mary Dagg, former tenants on the Fitzwilliam estate, were also on the 'Ticonderoga'. The letter 's' was added to their surname as well. Family tradition states that William arrived in America accompanied by his sister Eliza and a brother whose name has been forgotten. The only Dagg apart from William who appeared on the passenger lists was 27-year-old Mary. Mary does not feature in the family's oral history. William married late in life to a much younger woman who was born in America. Her name was Martha Kirk and they had five children. William died a few months before the birth of the fifth child, a son who was named

According to his headstone, William Dagg was born in 1840, but according to the passenger list he was 23 in 1850, which makes his year of birth 1827.

James. It is possible that Mary was his first wife and she might have died soon after arriving in Fort Smith. William is shown in the 1860 as living in Euper's boarding house. It is equally possible that Mary was William's sister. The present generation of Daggs say that William moved to Slaytonville, which is approximately twenty miles south-west of Fort Smith, and is buried near Sugarloaf Mountain south of Hartford. Eliza, which according to family tradition was the name of William's sister, married Captain Hugh Rogers.[25] Rogers and Andrew Hendricks became close friends and they frequently indulged in that most Irish of pastimes – a day at the races – at Jenny Lind Track in Fort Smith.[26]

Thirty-six-year-old Bryan Keefe had his family with him as well. His wife, Mary, was thirty-four and son John was fourteen. The O'Keefe headstone can be seen in Calvary Cemetery.

Another 'Ticonderoga' family were the Keatings. James Keating was a forty-year-old blacksmith. With him were his wife, Mary, who was ten years younger, their daughters Mary, eight, and Anne who was six. Mary jnr attended on the opening day of St Anne's Academy in Fort Smith which was established by the Sisters of

Mercy when they arrived in 1853. She later married James Coulter and after only four months together, they were separated by the Civil War for four years. Mary lived to a ripe old age and regaled family, friends and newspaper reporters with her memories of her young days in Fort Smith. She obviously never lost the gift of story-telling which was part-and-parcel of her Irish heritage.[27] The youngest was one-year-old Laurence. Mary had originally been a Kelly. Her parents and most of her brothers and sisters also sailed on the 'Ticonderoga'.

The Kelly family consisted of Tobias, his wife Mary, sons James, Nicholas and George and daughters Betty and Biddy. Their oldest son, Patrick, decided to stay in County Wicklow. Where the Kellys went or what they did after arrival in the United States is something of a mystery. Family tradition states that they may have stopped off in either Roseville or Clarkesville, east of Fort Smith, but fifty-one year old Tobias and his wife Mary and their family of five children do not appear in the 1850, 1860, 1870 or 1880 Arkansas census returns. Tobias and Mary had another son, Tobias jnr, and this is where a minor mystery presents itself. For some reason, Tobias jnr didn't wait for the rest of Hore's group which, as we have seen, left Ireland in October. It appears that he sailed on the 'Empire Queen' about three months earlier, arriving in New Orleans on September 4th 1850.[28] Tobias jnr settled in Fort Smith and what a varied life he had when he got there.

The Kelly brothers – including Patrick who remained in Ireland – were all butchers by trade, and Tobias jnr engaged in buying and butchering cattle and pigs in America. In 1862, he felt that the time had come for him to enlist and on August 17th, he joined Captain Luney Brewner Company, 1st Regiment Creek Mounted Volunteers, Confederate States of America at Cloaska, Cherokee Nation (now Oklahoma). He survived the war and in 1866 he married Mary Neville, fathering fourteen children. It appears that he later tried his hand at prospecting in Colorado in the 1870s but returned to Fort Smith in 1883. The family was later to establish a butcher business called "Kelly & Son, Dealers in Fresh Meats".[29] This business eventually passed into the Hendrick family, descendants of Andrew Hendrick and Margaret Breen, 'Ticonderoga' passengers. James, who had travelled on the 'Ticonderoga', later moved to Salt Lake City and became chief meat inspector for the state of Utah.

Another Irishman who resided in Fort Smith and who lived a full life was Michael Harrington. Harrington had been born at Berehaven, County Cork in 1829 and emigrated to America at the age of seventeen. He made his way west and began working as a teamster and later made his living as a stage coach driver and pilot. As pilot, it was his responsibility to guide government wagon trains across Indian Territory out into the far west and south-west outposts. In later life, he regaled his grandchildren and great grandchildren with stories of his adventures which included brushes with Indians and desperadoes as he drove the stage coach from Texas to Tucson, Arizona, probably the wildest part of the United States at that time. During the Civil War, he served under Colonel Cabell and at the cessation of hostilities he settled down in Fort Smith where he became a policeman. He spent the rest of his life there, dying at the age of 85.[30]

The level of interest Fort Smith residents have in the early Irish settlers is amazing and begs the question how much greater would it have been had Bishop Byrne's plans become reality? As it is, the few families who did settle there instilled a strong sense of their Irish identity into their descendants. Had the colonisation attempt succeeded, Fort Smith would have been Arkansas's Boston.

CHAPTER 11

Plan B

Thomas Hore must have been a bitterly disappointed man as he left Fort Smith. His plans for a strong, vibrant Irish colony in Arkansas had come to nothing. Only a few families had settled there. It was a demoralising outcome, but he couldn't afford to spend any time wallowing in self-recrimination or in useless rage against fate. There were 'hundreds'[1] of his flock waiting for him in St Louis. Besides, he had Plan B to put into action. Arkansas hadn't worked out, but there was still Iowa.

Thomas Carey had been one of the people who felt that he could not allow his family to run the risk of contracting fever in Little Rock. With his wife Peggy, he brought his five children to St Louis.[2] Dennis Murphy and his wife, Anne, did the same for their seven children. Their flight from Little Rock, and the flight of all the others, was perfectly understandable. For them, Little Rock and Arkansas promised nothing but more of the horrors they had left behind in Ireland. They believed that St Louis had to be different.

St Louis was a city which took itself very seriously. It was, perhaps, the greatest centre through which people passed as they travelled into the great open spaces of the plains and beyond. It was indeed the 'Gateway to the West'. It stood on the two mightiest rivers in North America, the Mississippi and the Missouri. The latter had wound its way for two thousand miles through Montana, the Dakotas, Nebraska, Kansas and across the state which adopted its name. From St Louis, pioneers could travel to almost anywhere. That was something it shared with Fort Smith, but that was all it shared. The inhabitants of the great city, particularly those with money, would claim they had more of the sophistication of the east than the rawness of the frontier. The local newspapers carried a profusion of advertisements for schools for the daughters of St Louis society. J Durkan's was only one of several 'English & Classical High Schools' vying for business. Every day the Sligo book store advertised its goods.[3] This was a city that had come a long way in a short time.

Up to 1820, St Louis had been little more than a village. Its first inhabitants took up residence in the mid-1760s and were French

St Louis' role in the "Push-West" is commemorated by the Gateway Arch. Beneath it is a museum depicting the mass movement of pioneers towards the Plains, the Rockies and California. Small elevators take visitors up through the arch to an observation gallery at the top.

Canadians who had moved south and Creoles who had come north from New Orleans. Shortly after the beginning of the nineteenth century about one hundred Irish business and professional men moved into the locality. Many were veterans of the French army and were readily integrated with the local people. It was these Irish immigrants who gave the town its first millionaire, sheriff and publisher.[4] From 1820 there was rapid expansion as Irish and German immigrants flooded in. In 1830, the population had jumped to 5,852, twenty years later, when Hore's group arrived, there were 160,773 people living in the city, over half of whom were immigrants. In 1860, 60% of the population had been born outside the United States. St Louis was America's premier 'immigrant' city.[5]

The Germans were the biggest ethnic group with 22,517. They outnumbered the next biggest, the Irish, almost two-to-one. Many of the Germans were Catholic, but this was no incentive to good relations between them and the Irish. In fact, German Catholics stayed away from other Germans and other Catholics of different nationalities. The same was true in Fort Smith where the German and Irish Catholics erected two different churches near to each other.

Many of the Irish in St Louis were paupers and lived in a district called 'Kerry Patch'. It was a shanty town. Some of their countrymen, however, were well-to-do and in 1842 an Irishman had been elected mayor. As had happened in other cities in America, some of the better-off Irish frowned on the influx of their pauper compatriots. Others, however, organised charities such as the Irish Emigration Society. This society was established to alleviate the suffering and distress of immigrants who were penniless and their services were in constant demand. In the opening months of 1851, they provided relief of one kind or another to 376 Irish people. At the O'Fallon Medical Dispensary, 1700 of the 2268 charity patients had been born in Ireland.[6] Not surprisingly, the arrival of another three hundred or so Irish immigrants didn't merit a mention in the local paper. They simply arrived and sought whatever accommodation there was or whatever they could afford. Once settled, they awaited the arrival of Fr Hore.

Hore made his way to them as quickly as he could and told them that he was going further upriver to Dubuque to investigate the land opportunities in Iowa. They were to stay in Missouri and he would come back for them as soon as he had things sorted out.

Once again, he found himself on a steamer on the Mississippi. One of the towns he passed on the port side was Hannibal where a young man named Samuel Clemens was beginning his working life in his brother's newspaper. Clemens was later to immortalise the river and its steam-boat culture under the pen-name of Mark Twain. The steamer continued on to Keokuk and on further still to Dubuque. It was here, on January 23rd, that Fr Hore disembarked and once again began his search for a suitable home for the people who had trusted in him to do just that.

As soon as he left the city, he headed south-east and continued for about twelve miles until he came to the monastery of Our Lady of La Trappe. This was New Melleray which the Cistercians of Waterford had opened two years previously. The prior there was Fr Francis Walshe, who had been prior in the Co Waterford house and was, in all probability, known to Fr Hore.

Hore used the monastery as a base from which to explore the countryside in search of land. There was nothing in the immediate area and he spread his net further. At some stage he heard of land about one hundred miles to the north. This was in Allamakee County at the extreme northeast of the state, bordering Minnesota. About six miles inland from Harper's Ferry, he stopped when he came to a wooded valley in a landscape that reminded him of his old parish in Co Wicklow. This was it. This was where he would bring his people. This was where the Irish colony would be established. He immediately returned to Dubuque and, in the Land Registry on February 22nd, he purchased over a thousand acres at $1.25 per acre. This property was parcelled out in seven lots, spread over two townships. There were six lots of 160 acres each in Lafayette township and one in Taylor township of 177 acres. The following day, he bought a further 700 acres in the same townships at the same price. In total, he spent $2296.25 for 1,837 acres of land – and he hadn't finished yet. He went back to New Melleray and told Fr Walshe of his find, then he boarded a riverboat yet again. For the first time since arriving in the United States on December 3rd, he was heading south.

On his arrival in St Louis, he gathered the families together and told them that their search was over, he had found them the land he had promised them. Their reaction was not what he expected. During his weeks in Iowa, many of them had found employment in the city and a place to stay. They were content to remain where they were.[7] Only eighteen families gathered their belongings and followed him.[8] Many of them did so out of family loyalty.

Tradition has it that they travelled upriver on the steamer 'Franklin', arriving at Lafayette Landing – a few miles north of Harper's Ferry, on March 25th, over three months after reaching New Orleans and a little more than five months since leaving Liverpool.[9] It was colder this far north than it had been in Arkansas and Missouri, but it was fresher with a healthy crispness that had been lacking down south, particularly in the cities. This was what these people had been used to and they headed towards the valley with optimism.

As he watched the eighteen families disembark and assemble their belongings, Thomas Hore must have thought of all the others who had gone their separate ways. Instead of twelve hundred people in Iowa, there was less than one hundred. Over one thousand others who had started the journey from Ireland were now scattered in the southern states and the mid-west. What had become of those who had sailed on the 'Chasca' and the 'Loodianah', he had no idea. Neither did he know how they were faring in New Orleans, Little Rock, Fort Smith or St Louis. As far as the Refugio-bound group was concerned, he would never know that they didn't reach the Texas township. He knew only the fates of those who had followed him to Iowa and of those who had died along the way.

Although Hore acquired the land at a bargain price, $1.25 an acre, the United States Government was still making quite a profit on it. According to one source, they had bought it from the native tribes for less than ten cents an acre.[10] The principal tribe in the area was the Winnebago. Although there had been little resistance to the 'push west' by the whites, the native Americans in this region did react on a few occasions. The most notable of these was known as the Black Hawk War which was fought mostly in Illinois and Wisconsin in 1832. Black Hawk and his people were forced west across the Mississippi into Iowa and Minnesota and over the

As bursar of New Melleray, Fr Bernard McCaffrey would also have been aware of financial transactions between the monastery and Fr Hore.

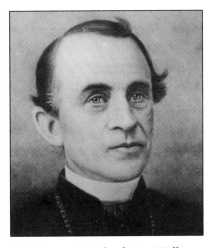

Fr Clement Smith of New Melleray. He worked closely with Fr Hore in land acquisition in Iowa. He later became Bishop of Dubuque.

next twenty years, not only did they lose title to their ancestral lands to the east but they were pushed even further west until they ended up in Montana. Their Iowa holdings were bought for the nominal price of ten cents by the federal government who then re-sold to settlers at $1.25. Now, to capitalise on the cheap land were the Heatleys, Heyfrons[11], Brickleys, Bolgers, Murphys, Esmonds and a few others[12]. To make sure that each family had enough land to make it viable, Hore purchased another two plots of 160 acres each on April 16th. This was his last purchase, bringing his total to 2,157 acres. They were not the first white settlers in the area. One local historian believes that Fr Hore's group were the third contingent to arrive.[13] There was already a French colony in the vicinity and these welcomed the Irish arrivals, opening their homes to them until the newcomers had their own houses erected.[14] Not surprisingly, one of the first tasks of the group was the construction of a parish church. There is evidence to show that some sort of church had been either in existence or construction had begun as early as 1848. The centenary of the parish was celebrated in 1948 and there was also a transom in the original church which bore the inscription "Donated by Michael Mooney 1848", yet local tradition states that Fr Hore frequently said mass outdoors.[15] One way or the other, a good deal of work was needed before the group had a satisfactory place of worship. When the church was completed, they dedicated it to St George. This would indicate that construction finished on April 23rd, the saint's feast day.

When the families had settled and a recognisable community had been established, the time had come to name it. William Heatley suggested the name of Wexford and this has led to some confusion ever since. Many of those who had travelled with Fr Hore had been his parishioners in south County Wicklow – Heatley himself was from Rathdrum in County Wicklow – but Hore was a native of County Wexford and some of his relatives had travelled from County Wexford with him to America. Other Wexford natives also joined the large group of emigrants. In was in deference to the priest's leadership that the name Wexford was proposed.

The Heatleys were to claim two 'firsts' in the parish history. On May 25th, 1851 – just a month after the completion of the church, Mary Ann Heatley became the first child to be baptised there. She was the daughter of William and Elizabeth and her sponsors had also been 'Ticonderoga' passengers, Edward Stafford

The present church, Immaculate Conception, at Wexford, Iowa. The names on the surrounding headstones bear testimony to the community's Irish origins

and Mary Heyfron. At the other end of the scale, William Heatley became the first person to be buried in the churchyard.

Another of the 'Ticonderoga' families which led prominent lives in the new Wexford were the Bolgers – or Bulgers, both spellings have been used to denote the same family. They were John and Catherine (or Kate), Michael, Pat, Fanny, Mary and Ellen. John died in or around 1852, but Catherine survived for another twenty years. Family tradition has it that Patrick was famous in Ireland as a tap dancer. He could "dance on a plate without breaking it" and is said to have danced for Queen Victoria prior to his leaving Ireland. Michael, according to one account, was a large man. So large that when he reached old age and became a victim of senility he survived without eating for fifty days before his death. His epitaph epitomises the true qualities of the Irish emigrant:

"Of the pioneers of the early fifties none pursued their vocations of honest and industrious agricultural toil with more diligence than did those brawny frontiersmen, the Bolger brothers, and they succeeded well."

Another family tradition concerns the sisters Fanny and Mary. Mary was in love with a young man named Miles Roach (his surname would indicate that he was also of Wexford, Ireland origin or descent). He came one day to ask here to the circus, but when he arrived she had gone on an errand. Fanny entertained him and he had to leave before Mary returned. As a joke, Fanny told Mary that Miles had asked her to go to the circus instead. Mary became angry and never forgave her sister. She left home shortly thereafter and never returned. Mary died young and when her body was brought back for the funeral, Fanny begged them to open the casket so that she could make her peace. Perhaps that was why Fanny never married. She died in 1899.[16]

Although Hore's jurisdiction was quite extensive – he being the only priest in Allamakee County – the number of Catholics in the area was small. Despite births within the group and the influx of other settlers, many of whom were Irish Catholics eager to be 'among their own', there were only 153 Catholics at Wexford and a mere 257 in the entire county in 1852. Hore reported to the bishop that there were not enough children there to require catechism classes. As word of the Catholic settlement spread,

Michael Bolger seen here with his wife Mary (Manton) who was originally from Co. Waterford. They were married in 1861.

however, more Catholic settlers came into the area, as the diocesan administration had hoped would be the case – just as Bishop Byrne in Little Rock had hoped would be the case in Arkansas. Within a year the number of people Hore could count as his parishioners trebled. The new settlers came from other states. Many had been in America before the arrival of Fr Hore and his group. Some had been born in America to Irish immigrants and had moved from the east, from New York and Illinois. Some came north from Louisiana and Kentucky. Others, of course, were 'fresh off the boat' from ports in Ireland or Britain. By 1855 there were enough children to warrant a school at Wexford and it was becoming obvious that the small timber-frame church was inadequate. Sometime in the late 1850s a new, larger structure was erected. This was also dedicated to St George. It was later re-dedicated to the Immaculate Conception.

From the time of their arrival, throughout this period of growth, Fr Hore kept in regular contact with the monastery of New Melleray. On the day he made his last purchase of land, April 16th, he also loaned $490 to the monastery. The monks were having financial trouble having suffered two successive crop failures[17]. Their difficulties would seem to have been no more than cash-flow problems as they repaid the loan five weeks later. Over the next couple of years, there were other, smaller loans, which also appear to have been repaid. More intriguing is the fact that between 1852 and 1857, Thomas Hore deeded 951 acres to the monastery for a total sum of $3112, but not a cent of this sum changed hands.

Thomas Hore was not interested in owning land in Iowa. When the third and final transaction was made, in 1857, plans were immediately set in motion to establish a branch house at Wexford. About a month after the arrival of the monks in the valley, Fr Hore said his goodbyes and headed home. He was sixty years of age and he had done what many men half his age would not have contemplated doing. It is very unlikely that he ever intended spending the rest of his life in America. Yet, he could not bring himself to return to Ireland without first making sure that the people who had followed him so far would have easy access to the sacraments of the church to which they owed their allegiance. By transferring his land to the monastery of New Melleray he ensured that his parishioners would always have clergymen close at hand to look after their spiritual needs.

Window in the Immaculate Conception Church, Wexford, Iowa.

Conclusion

By the time Fr Hore decided to return home, the families he had taken to America had settled in and were busy getting on with their lives. No doubt, they thought of Ireland often and tried to keep in touch with what was happening 'at home'. The scene of Andrew Hendrick reading the "Boston Pilot" to his neighbours was probably repeated in the other centres in which the splinter groups ended up. Letters, sometimes written by the local priest, would be brought by ship back to Ireland and replies, taking weeks at best, would bring everyone 'up-to-date' with family news. Many of the letters 'home' would include hard-earned cash to enable other family members and friends to save for a ticket so they, too, could share in the rewards of labour. This strength of family unity was one of the greatest virtues displayed by the Irish abroad.

With time, the memories of the famine and repression would fade. They would be either twisted into a bitter hatred or tinged with nostalgia. Either way, the stories passed on to descendants would shape their impressions of Ireland and the Irish people.

While many of the families remained in the locations they first settled in, many more became part of that most American of characteristics – mobility. A survey has shown that in the mixed ethnic city of St Louis, the majority of Irish immigrants were very mobile, usually changing their address at least once in the first few years of arrival in the United States. Perhaps they were continually looking for the end of the rainbow. Irish people could always be found where gold and silver were mined. And why not? When suffering in Ireland, they constantly heard of how everyone in America was 'doing well for themselves'. It was easy to fall into the trap of thinking that there was nothing to do but undertake the Atlantic crossing and then start making a fortune. They soon learned that this was not the case. A good life was to be had, but it

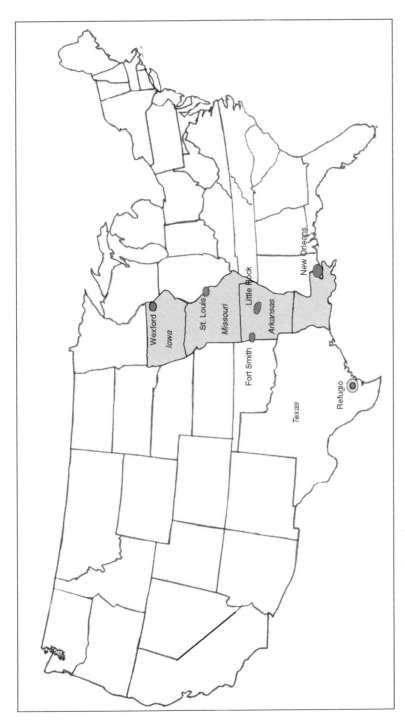

Where the splinter groups located.

was hard work and at times dangerous. In the cities, there was little opportunity to succeed as the scramble for housing and work daily increased. Anyone who made it to the top did so through single-minded ambition, like Scarlet O'Hara fired with the thought of 'never going hungry again'. In the countryside, back-breaking toil was the only way to turn virgin soil into cultivated land.

Little wonder that the sons of several of Fr Hore's group went to Colorado in search of silver in the 1870s. They were now part of the American dream and an essential part of that dream was the opportunity for everyone to make it rich. Others simply followed the push west as more land was taken from the Indians and put up for sale at low prices by the federal government.

When recalling what fate had in store for this group, perhaps the most poignant twist were the years of conflict which the northern states called the Civil War and which the southerners still refer to as the War Between The States. In that war, people who had travelled together with Thomas Hore found themselves on different sides. Those who settled in Louisiana and Arkansas donned the grey of the Confederacy; those who made their way to Missouri and Iowa fought in the blue of the Union. It is sad to think that one-time Wicklow and Wexford neighbours might have had each other in their rifle sights because of a quirk of providence.

There is still residue emotion from that conflict, particularly in the South. Nevertheless, the descendants of this group in New Orleans, Little Rock and Fort Smith know that they have a great deal in common with their fellow descendants in St Louis and Wexford, Iowa. They are very proud of what their ancestors did.Most Americans of Irish descent I have met – whether descended from this particular group or not – are proud of their Irish blood and, at times, carry their names like banners. Many have kept the Catholic faith, which they deem to be an inextricable part of their Irishness.The descendants of the Hore group feel this particularly, probably because Hore was a priest working for the bishop of Little Rock. In that instance, it would be extremely difficult to separate church and nationality.

And so, to the question: -Did Thomas Hore succeed?

That depends on what he was trying to achieve. If his aim was to

The church of Caim, where Fr Hore spent a year before being appointed parish priest of Cloughbawn.

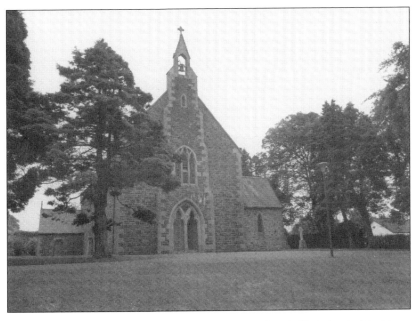

The church at Cloughbawn which Fr Hore completed. He is buried inside.

establish two flourishing Irish Catholic colonies in Arkansas – one in Little Rock, the other in Fort Smith – the answer, obviously, is no. But if his aim was to take people out of a nightmare in Ireland and to give them a better chance of a decent life, the answer has got to be yes. He brought them to a country which was growing. Perhaps the moral issues involved in buying land from the federal government – land which had been taken from the Indians despite repeated treaties – could, and should, be called into question. Nevertheless, Hore's first allegiance was to the people he encouraged to leave Ireland.

It can also be argued that his success rate was dismal even in this, because less than forty families settled where he asked them to settle in Arkansas or Iowa – less than forty, out of an estimated four hundred. The answer to that lies in the fact that at no time did Hore compel anyone to go where they did not want to go. Those who stayed in other places, such as New Orleans and St Louis, did so of their own volition. Those who headed west towards Refugio also went of their own free will and Hore should not be called upon to answer for their fates. Those who stuck to his plans, he looked after as best he could. As a priest, he was responsible for their spiritual well-being. In Little Rock and Fort Smith, he knew that Bishop Byrne and his priests would be on hand to minister the sacraments. In Iowa, he made it possible for the monks of New Melleray to establish a religious colony in Wexford. It was only after he was satisfied that this venture was getting under way did he take his leave of his people. This was one aspect he had to be sure of before heading back to Ireland alone and, no doubt, beginning to feel his age.

The measure of success is always subjective. In my opinion, Thomas Hore succeeded.

Fr Hore's Last Years

On his return to Ireland, Fr Hore once more worked in the diocese of Ferns. Before taking up his duties, however, he made a pligrimage to the Holy Land and was away for several months. On his return he was appointed curate at Caim, County Wexford. On August 28th, 1859 he was again promoted to parish priest and was given the responsibility of Cloughbawn where the most urgent task was the completion of a new parish church.

Thomas Hore had done enough to merit a few quiet years before he died and, perhaps, he found that peace and quiet in Cloughbawn. On June 14th, 1864 he died and a few days later was buried inside the church. His passing was marked by a high mass attended by forty priests. Inside the church is a tablet with the following inscription:

"Of Your Charity/Pray for the happy repose/of the soul/of the Rev. Thomas Hore/P.P.Cloughbawn/who departed this life/the 14th day of June 1864/ in the 69th year of his age/May the almighty God/have mercy on his soul/amen".

The Monastery at Wexford, Iowa

The reason behind the attempted establishment of a second monastery in Iowa was to accommodate the wholesale transfer of monks from Mount Melleray in Ireland. As we have seen, this would appear to have been Dom Bruno Fitzpatrick's intention as early as 1848. The arrival of Fr Hore and his group in Iowa and the subsequent acquisiton of the land by the monastery from Hore was all the monks could have wished for. But several factors worked against them and the Wexford monastery never became a reality. One of these factors was that the prior, Fr Walsh, was expected to establish and run the new branch house with five lay brothers as well as tend to the pastoral needs of the local laity after Fr Hore's departure. It was simply too much responsibility. The most important factor, however, lay back in Ireland. Just as the new monastery at Wexford was getting under way, Dom Fitzpatrick's plans to move lock, stock and barrel to America were defeated. There was, therefore, no need to have a second house in Iowa. Fr Walsh asked to be dispensed from the order and he devoted himself to pastoral work at Wexford until 1860. He later worked in other parishes before his death in 1893.

The land at Wexford was later sold off in lots to local farmers.

Bishop Byrne's Arkansas Colonies

Despite the disastrous attempt to transplant hundreds of Irish Catholics in Little Rock and Fort Smith under the guidance of Fr Hore, Bishop Byrne pressed on. A quick comparison of the entry for the diocese in the 1851 Catholic Directory with that of the following year displays his determination.

Much of the activity was in the hands of the Sisters of Mercy who accompanied him hot on the heels of Fr Hore's group and their contribution to the strengthening and spread of Catholicism in the diocese cannot be overstated. Nonetheless, the bishop was a man who led by example and the strain of overwork began to take its toll. The added strain of trying to work impartially in the midst of civil war in the 1860s drained him of his last energies and he died at the Sister of Mercy convent in Helena on June 10th, 1860. He was 57 years old.

APPENDIX 1

The Refugio Connection

At first glance it seems strange that a contingent of Hore's group should suddenly decide to head even further west than Arkansas. What could possibly attract them to a remote settlement in the wilds of Texas in a land where the local Indians, the Karankawa, were still hostile towards invasion of their territory?

The answer lies in the fact that there was a colony of people already there who had emigrated from north Wexford and surrounding districts twenty years earlier.

It had all started with a man from the north Wexford village of Ballygarrett named James Power. Power was born in 1789. During his formative years he had experienced the riots against the unfair impositon of Church Tithes on Catholics, he lived through the bloody rebellion of 1798 and witnessed the heartless recriminations of the authorities in its aftermath. By the time he reached the age of twenty-one, he had decided that Ireland had nothing to offer ambitious young men and he sailed to America. He landed at Philadelphia, but the following year he moved to New Orleans where he became a successful merchant. After twelve years of shrewd business, he decided to head west and invest his capital. For some reason he chose the Mexican city of Saltillo, almost two hundred miles south of the present Texas border, and again set up as a merchant but also traded in mining equipment. It was here in the following year, 1823, that he met a fellow Irishman, James Hewetson from Thomastown, County Kilkenny.

Mexico was a new political entity at this time. It had won its independence from Spain in 1821 and its territory included what is now the state of Texas. Four years later a decision was made to populate that region and both Power and Hewetson, along with two other Irishmen, John McMullan and James McGloin, applied to the government to act as impressarios (agents) to bring in settlers. They proposed to bring in four hundred people (three hundred of whom would be Irish and one hundred Mexican). They assured the government that the settlers would be 'laborious, of good habits and morals, of the Roman Catholic and Apostolic religion'. It took eighteen months to get permission but only two hundred settlers would be allowed and half of these were to be Mexican. There were to be two colonies, one with its centre at Refugio, the other at San Patricio. Power lived in Refugio and shared responsibility of that colony with Hewetson. The San Patricio colony was the responsibility of McMullan and McGloin. Five years later, Hewetson left Power in sole charge of their enterprise after he married a wealthy widow in Saltillo and decided to look after her business interests there (now his by marriage). Power immediately headed back to Ireland to recruit as many Irish people as he could to develop 'his' colony as he felt it should be developed.

It had been twenty years since he had left Ballygarrett, and his arrival caused a stir. There was even more excitement when he put up posters all over the county and neighbouring counties proclaiming his intention to lead them to a country that would be their salvation. All they needed was $30 for the fare and land fees which would give them title to tillage farms of 177 acres or ranches to breed livestock covering 4428 acres. Such dimensions were mind-boggling to people who eked their existance on farms of five or ten acres. An estimated two hundred and fifty families could not resist the opportunity.

They first went to Liverpool and, from there, sailed to New Orleans, from there they sailed in two chartered schooners across the Gulf of Mexico to Port Aransas. The final stage was overland to Refugio. It had been a nightmare of a journey. Not only were the usual hardships of ocean travel experienced but as they approached the Texas shore, the schooners grounded and were wrecked with the loss of all the passengers' possessions. As well as this, cholera broke out. To top it all was the growing mutual unease with which the Mexican government and the European-American settlers viewed each other. This was to erupt into rebellion by the settlers against the government, the establishment of a short-lived Texas republic and eventual integration into the United States.

For some of Power's group, it was all too much and a few returned to New Orleans where they undoubtedly still were when Hore's group arrived in 1850.

It is inconceivable that at least some of this later batch of emigrants were not aware of a Wexford colony in Refugio, particularly as it was only established less than two decades previously. Some of the later group were in all probability related to members of the earlier group. It is also more than likely that they met some of Power's group who had returned to New Orleans. Under these circumstances, is it unreasonable that so many decided to carry on towards a township where they would be made welcome as fellow countrymen, if not countymen? After all, they knew nobody in Arkansas.

The story of James Power and the Refugio Irish has been written by Richard Roche in his book "The Texas Connection".

The Melleray Connection, Iowa:

Dom Bruno Fitzpatrick was anxious to establish a new house of the Melleray monastery in the United States. According to Schmitz it would appear that Fr Hore was a visitor to Mount Melleray during the time that this search for a location of a new house in America was being undertaken. He would therfore have been well aware of it. He would also have been aware that the search was successfully concluded in July 1849 when a tract of land twelve miles south-west of Dubuque, Iowa was chosen on which to build the new monastery of Our Lady of La Trappe of New Melleray. It was again more than likely that he was also aware of the fact that the prior of Mount Melleray in Waterford had arrived in Dubuque on April 12th, 1850 as the prior to the new monastery – just six months before Fr Hore left Ireland for Arkansas.

In the collection of papers pertaining to Archbishop Cullen in the Dublin Diocesan Archives are a number of letters referring to great unrest in Mount Melleray. The first in the series of twelve, dated between January and October 1851, alludes to "three defectors" who should not be sent to America. Perusal of the other letters show how several members of the Melleray community accused Dom Bruno, the abbot, of inciting the monks, lay-workers and neighbouring farmers to join the rebellion against English rule in what was known as the Young Ireland rebellion in 1848. They said that they objected to such behaviour. Other monks, they claimed, actually began preparing to take part in what proved to be a very abortive attempt at rebellion – it was hardly more than an isolated skirmish. These preparations, they admitted, took place when Abbot Fitzpatrick was away, so they could not state that he had been actively involved in these preparations. On his return, however, he took the conspirators under his wing, protecting them from the accusations of those monks who refused to participate in proposed outrage against the government. Not only that, they claimed, but the abbot made life for his accusers extremely difficult. They also made the claim that it was Fitzpatrick's intention to close the monastery and move everyone to Iowa.

Because of the abbot's vengeful spirit, they said, they could no longer remain in the monastery and left to establish a new house at Prospect Hill, Dublin.

Over the next few months they appealed to the archbishop to recognise their goodwill and to grant them permission to form a new community, independent of Dom Fitzpatrick and the Mount Melleray regime. This was denied, but it was agreed that a visit to Melleray was called for to assess the situation.

Archbishop Cullen reported that "no Superior of a religious house can profess more fully or more justly the confidence and respect of his community than does the Abbot of this monastery, the Right Reverend Father Bruno Fitzpatrick". The report went on to say that the break-away faction had been misguided. A second visit of inspection and subsequent report by an abbot from England and an abbot from France came to the same conclusion. It would then appear that Cullen appealed to the abbot to allow the miscreants back into the community, but Dom Bruno was adamant. He neither wanted the break-aways back in Waterford nor in the new house in Iowa.

The last letter of the twelve, however, is from one of the 'miscreants' who had left Melleray on account of the treatment he received because of his opposition to Dom Bruno's way of doing things. He was Fr Cosgrave. His letter describes his long, arduous journey which he could not have completed had it not been for the kindness of an Irish Protestant gentleman who paid his stagecoach fare for the last portion of the journey. On his arrival at New Melleray, however, he was not allowed in. The letter preserved in the Dublin Diocesan Archives is to Rev and Mrs Dooley (presumably the Protestant gentleman referred to in the letter) asking that he intercede with the monastery on his behalf.

I could find no reply and know nothing of Cosgrave's fate.

APPENDIX 2

The Emigrants

The following is a list of passengers on board the 'Ticonderoga', the 'Loodianah' and the 'Chasca'. The names are listed alphabetically and not in the order in which they appeared in the original passenger lists. Where families have been identified, a code has been allocated. To identify the members of a family, for example that of Loughlin Byrne, simply use the code column to locate other names which have the same code number. Identification was made primarily through groupings of names on the lists.

It is possible that some of the passengers were members of identified families but were not coded with them as they were separated from the group on the list. For example, Robert Carey might have been a member of family #84. Some passengers were separated from families with a similar surname by only one other passenger. In such cases, and in the absence of other data, I decided to err on the side of caution and withold family identification. On the other hand, the names of John and Julia Kenny (family #135) were separated on the passenger list by one name but the discovery of John and Julia in the St Louis census of 1860 confirmed a family relationship. In the census the spelling of the name had changed to Kenney. Also in St Louis, Mary Goslin became Mary Gosling and Philip McDonnell became Philip McDonald.

Spelling variations were very common in the last century and should not outweigh other identification factors. It is likely that Andrew Sennett, Anne Sinnett and Catherine Sinnott were members of one family. The difference in spelling could be accounted for by their giving their names, either on the ship or at the point of disembarkation, to different enumerators who spelled the name as they heard it, but I could find no supporting evidence for this except for the close proximity of the names on the passenger list. Likewise, it will be noticed that Kelly was also spelt Kelley; Brien (or O'Brien) was spelt Bryan; Fennel spelt with one l and two ll's, and Kavanagh could be Kavanah, Kavanaugh, Cavanagh, etc. In all cases, the names have been spelt as they appeared on the lists. Therefore, Catherine Lloyd appears as Catherine Loyd.

One final point regarding identification. Some of the names on the passenger lists were illegible. Others were difficult to decipher and one or two names may be incorrect, but the vast majority of names were easily identifiable.

Discovering where families and individuals settled was achieved mainly through contact with descendant families and U.S. 1860 census returns. The intervening nine years between the immigrants' arrival and the census meant that many of them had moved on to pastures new. This was particluarly true of many of those who went to St Louis, the 'Gateway to the West'. In some cases, where the parents of a young family (that is, 'young' in 1850) have been traced in the census nine years later but the children do not appear, the assumption has been made that the children accompanied the parents to those locations in 1850/1 but may have moved on as they grew older. Young females, of course, could have remained in the area in which they originally settled but could not be positively identified because of change of surname through marriage.

Another problem was the proliferation of some names, such as Mary Murphy and James Byrne. It was relatively easy to find correponding names and ages in the 1860 census, but because of the popularity of such names, it simply was not possible to make positive identification in all cases.

One last point, Thom Gardner's age was more likely to be 19 rather than 79, but the first digit looked more like 7 than 1 on the photocopy of the passenger list from which the information came.

Many of the passengers on the "Ticonderoga" (and, presumably, the other ships as well) travelled on multiple contract tickets. For example, on Ticket No. 22 (16), the following fourteen passengers were named: John Bulger, Kate Bulger, Fanny Bulger, Margaret Doyle, Catherine Doyle, Edmund Murphy, Thomas McManus, Michael Kincella, James Kincella, Daniel Finn, Margaret Sheridan, Edward Stafford, Frank Murphy, and George Murphy. The total cost of that ticket was £70 or £5 per passenger.

LIST OF MIGRANTS

Surname	First name	Age	Ship	Location	Code
?	?	25	Chasca		
?	Betty	27	Chasca		104
?	Bridget	38	Chasca		101
?	Bridget	8	Chasca		101
?	Ellen	20	Chasca		
?	Maria	11	Chasca		101
?	Mary	25	Chasca		104
?	Thomas	17	Chasca		101
ACIDIS	Margaret	25	Chasca		115
ACIDIS	Robert	24	Chasca		115
ALLEY	June	26	Chasca		86
ALLEY	William	20	Chasca		86
ANDERSON	Jessey	24	Chasca		
ARTON	P	23	Loodianah		
BAHAN	M	23	Loodianah		
BAILY	Anne	21	Ticonderoga		80
BAILY	Catherine	18	Ticonderoga		80
BAILY	Ellen	51	Ticonderoga		80
BAILY	Michael	23	Ticonderoga		80
BAMBRECK	Thom	22	Chasca		
BARRET	Ellen	18	Chasca		
BARRETT	Jeremiah	35	Chasca		
BARRY	Mary	21	Chasca		
BARRY	Peter	30	Ticonderoga		
BEHAN	John	23	Loodianah		
BEHAN	Patrick		Ticonderoga	Little Rock	
BICKELE	William	30	Chasca		
BOGGAN	John	30	Ticonderoga		40
BOGGAN	Patrick	25	Ticonderoga		40
BOLAND	John	14	Chasca		
BOLGER	Edward	21	Ticonderoga		69
BOLGER	Michael	21	Ticonderoga		69
BOWIN	Elisabeth	22	Chasca		
BRADY	Peter	28	Chasca		
BRASS	P	24	Loodianah		

Surname	First name	Age	Ship	Location	Code
BREEN	Anne	20	Ticonderoga	Fort Smith	32
BREEN	Fanny	53	Ticonderoga	Fort Smith	32
BREEN	James	57	Ticonderoga	Fort Smith	32
BREEN	John	22	Ticonderoga	Fort Smith	32
BREEN	Margaret		Ticonderoga	Fort Smith	32
BREEN	Mary	13	Ticonderoga	Fort Smith	32
BREEN	Patrick	18	Ticonderoga	Fort Smith	32
BREEN	Peter	18	Ticonderoga	Fort Smith	32
BREEN	William	9	Ticonderoga	Fort Smith	32
BRENNAN	Catherine	22	Ticonderoga	Little Rock	55
BRENNAN	Catherine	50	Ticonderoga	Little Rock	55
BRENNAN	James	14	Ticonderoga	Little Rock	55
BRENNAN	John	14	Ticonderoga	Little Rock	55
BRENNAN	Jon	34	Chasca		
BRENNAN	Michael	35	Chasca		
BRENNAN	Mogue	60	Ticonderoga	Little Rock	55
BRENNAN	Patrick	25	Ticonderoga	Little Rock	55
BRENNAN	Thomas	20	Ticonderoga	Little Rock	55
BRIAN	C	22	Loodianah		
BRIAN	J	27	Loodianah		
BRIAN	James	26	Loodianah		143
BRIAN	James	28	Loodianah		
BRIAN	Thomas	25	Loodianah		143
BRICKLEY	Bess		Ticonderoga		29
BRICKLEY	Daniel	25	Ticonderoga	Wexford	18
BRICKLEY	James	56	Ticonderoga	Wexford	18
BRICKLEY	John	30	Ticonderoga		
BRICKLEY	Mary	48	Ticonderoga		29
BRICKLEY	Paul	36	Ticonderoga	Wexford	18
BRICKLEY	Richard	21	Ticonderoga		29
BRICKLEY	William	50	Ticonderoga		29
BRIEN	Catherine	25	Ticonderoga		54
BRIEN	Dennis	40	Ticonderoga		54
BRIEN	Honora	36	Chasca		
BRIEN	Martin	26	Chasca		
BRIEN	Matthew	26	Chasca		
BRIEN	Michael	35	Ticonderoga		54

Surname	First name	Age	Ship	Location	Code
BROWN	Elisabeth	22	Chasca		
BROWNE	Rose	22	Ticonderoga		
BRYAN	Biddy	25	Ticonderoga		82
BRYAN	Lucy	26	Ticonderoga		82
BULGER	Ellen	20	Ticonderoga	Wexford	6
BULGER	Fanny	25	Ticonderoga	Wexford	6
BULGER	James	27	Chasca		
BULGER	John	50	Ticonderoga	Wexford	6
BULGER	Kate	55	Ticonderoga	Wexford	6
BULGER	Mary	22	Ticonderoga	Wexford	6
BULGER	Michael	24	Ticonderoga	Wexford	6
BULGER	Patt	5	Ticonderoga	Wexford	6
BURKE	Mary	22	Ticonderoga	St Louis	
BURKE	Patt	31	Ticonderoga		
BUTLER	Sarah	22	Ticonderoga		
BYANT	James	25	Loodianah		
BYRNE	A	24	Loodianah		
BYRNE	Anne	12	Ticonderoga		63
BYRNE	Anne	60	Ticonderoga		34
BYRNE	Betsy	18	Ticonderoga		63
BYRNE	Betty	20	Ticonderoga		67
BYRNE	Betty	24	Ticonderoga		22
BYRNE	Biddy	17	Ticonderoga		58
BYRNE	Bridget		Ticonderoga		22
BYRNE	Charles	21	Ticonderoga		63
BYRNE	Charles	25	Ticonderoga		46
BYRNE	Eliza	1	Ticonderoga		67
BYRNE	Eliza	21	Ticonderoga		58
BYRNE	Ellen	19	Ticonderoga		58
BYRNE	Ellen	22	Ticonderoga		34
BYRNE	George	33	Ticonderoga		
BYRNE	H	26	Loodianah		
BYRNE	James	13	Ticonderoga		63
BYRNE	James	20	Loodianah		
BYRNE	James	20	Ticonderoga		22
BYRNE	James	21	Ticonderoga		41
BYRNE	James	22	Ticonderoga		

Surname	First name	Age	Ship	Location	Code
BYRNE	James	23	Ticonderoga		
BYRNE	James	60	Ticonderoga		63
BYRNE	John	25	Loodianah		
BYRNE	John	35	Chasca		
BYRNE	Laurence	16	Ticonderoga		63
BYRNE	Laurence	18	Chasca		
BYRNE	Laurence	24	Ticonderoga		
BYRNE	Loughlin	55	Ticonderoga		58
BYRNE	Mary	18	Ticonderoga		13
BYRNE	Mary	30	Ticonderoga		46
BYRNE	Mary	60	Ticonderoga		63
BYRNE	Michael	24	Ticonderoga		34
BYRNE	Michael	40	Ticonderoga		
BYRNE	Miles	30	Ticonderoga		13
BYRNE	Murtogh	60	Ticonderoga		34
BYRNE	Patrick	28	Ticonderoga		34
BYRNE	Patt	25	Chasca		
BYRNE	Patt	28	Ticonderoga		
BYRNE	Patt	40	Ticonderoga		67
BYRNE	Patt	51	Ticonderoga		22
BYRNE	Peggy	24	Ticonderoga		22
BYRNE	Richard	27	Ticonderoga		41
BYRNE	Rose	26	Ticonderoga		67
BYRNE	S	20	Loodianah		
BYRNE	Sally	14	Ticonderoga		63
BYRNE	William	20	Ticonderoga		34
BYRNE	William	24	Ticonderoga		
BYRNEY	G	25	Loodianah		
CAFFREY	Catherine	35	Ticonderoga		48
CAFFREY	Edward	28	Ticonderoga		48
CAHILL	Bridget	38	Chasca		97
CAHILL	John	36	Chasca		97
CAIN	Mary	18	Chasca		
CALLEN	James	15	Loodianah		136
CALLEN	John	20	Loodianah		136
CALLEN	John	48	Loodianah		136
CALLEN	M	16	Loodianah		136

Surname	First name	Age	Ship	Location	Code
CAREY	Anne	11	Ticonderoga	St Louis	84
CAREY	James	14	Ticonderoga	St Louis	84
CAREY	John	15	Ticonderoga	St Louis	
CAREY	Mary	21	Ticonderoga	St Louis	84
CAREY	Michael	25	Ticonderoga	St Louis	84
CAREY	Peggy	50	Ticonderoga	St Louis	84
CAREY	Robert	31	Ticonderoga		
CAREY	Thomas	19	Ticonderoga	St Louis	84
CAREY	Thomas	51	Ticonderoga	St Louis	84
CARNEY	Mary	20	Chasca		117
CARNEY	Mathew	22	Chasca		117
CARNEY	Robert	25	Chasca		117
CARTY	Michael	26	Chasca		
CASEY	Johanna	7	Chasca		111
CASEY	Mary	20	Chasca		111
CASEY	Patt	26	Chasca		
CASSEY	Johanna	21	Chasca		
CAULFIELD	John	26	Chasca		
CAULFIELD	John	7	Chasca		123
CAULFIELD	Mary	30	Chasca		123
CAVANNAH	P	40	Loodianah		
CHANEY	M	23	Loodianah		
CHRISTIE	James	24	Chasca		87
CHRISTIE	William	28	Chasca		87
CLINCH	Biddy	40	Ticonderoga		68
CLINCH	Eliza	14	Ticonderoga		68
CLINCH	Ellen	15	Ticonderoga		68
CLINCH	Mary	18	Ticonderoga		68
CLINCH	Michael	40	Ticonderoga		68
CODD	Nicholas	40	Ticonderoga		
COLLINS	Thom	30	Chasca		
CONDON	Cath	55	Chasca		
CONDON	Thos	16	Loodianah		
CONDRAN	Alexander	22	Ticonderoga		16
CONDRAN	Edward	24	Ticonderoga		16
CONDRAN	Mary	20	Ticonderoga		16
CONNOR	Patrick	24	Chasca		

Surname	First name	Age	Ship	Location	Code
CONNOR	Patt	18	Ticonderoga		
CONROY	Thomas	24	Chasca		
CONWAY	Thos	21	Chasca		
CORRAN	D	18	Loodianah		
COURTNEY	Margaret	19	Chasca		89
COURTNEY	Mary	40	Chasca		89
COUSENS	Anne	27	Ticonderoga		
CRAVIN	Bridget	16	Chasca		
CRAVIN	Honora	26	Chasca		
CRAVIN	Martin	28	Chasca		120
CRAVIN	Mary	19	Chasca		
CRAVIN	Michael	30	Chasca		120
CROW	John	28	Chasca		
CRUMSEE	George	22	Chasca		
CULLEN	Ambrose	27	Ticonderoga		72
CULLEN	Anne	11	Chasca		99
CULLEN	Anne	26	Ticonderoga		72
CULLEN	Bridget	34	Chasca		99
CULLEN	Honora	17	Chasca		99
CULLEN	James	6	Chasca		99
CULLEN	Jane	Inf	Chasca		99
CULLEN	Thomas	18	Chasca		99
CULNANE	Patt	25	Chasca		
CUSHION	Patt	30	Chasca		
DAGG	Mary	27	Ticonderoga	Fort Smith	134
DAGG	William	23	Ticonderoga	Fort Smith	134
DALTON	Anne	24	Ticonderoga		38
DALTON	Betty	24	Ticonderoga		31
DALTON	Margaret	11	Ticonderoga		31
DALTON	Michael	24	Chasca		
DALTON	Thomas	25	Ticonderoga		31
DALTON	Thomas	30	Ticonderoga		38
DANLEY	James	1	Loodianah		149
DANLEY	John	11	Loodianah		149
DARCY	Thom	23	Chasca		
DAWSON	Mary Jane	19	Chasca		133
DAWSON	Thomas	28	Chasca		133

Surname	First name	Age	Ship	Location	Code
DEMPSEY	Honora	30	Chasca		
DILLON	D	29	Loodianah		146
DILLON	Thos	30	Loodianah		146
DOHERTY	Catherine	35	Ticonderoga		15
DOHERTY	Tobias	20	Ticonderoga		15
DONIGAN	M	45	Loodianah		142
DONIGAN	P	13	Loodianah		142
DONIGAN	P	7	Loodianah		142
DONNERY	John	55	Ticonderoga		
DONOHUE	Bridget	30	Ticonderoga		3
DONOHUE	James	20	Ticonderoga		
DOHOHUE	Patt	26	Ticonderoga		
DONOHUE	Patt	27	Ticonderoga		3
DONOHUE	Patt	30	Ticonderoga		
DONOLY	P	46	Loodianah		
DORAN	Ann	21	Chasca		
DORAN	Biddy	24	Ticonderoga		51
DORAN	Dolly	24	Ticonderoga		51
DORAN	Miles	33	Chasca		
DORSAY	John	18	Ticonderoga		
DOWNEY	Mary	22	Ticonderoga		
DOWNEY	William	65	Loodianah		
DOYLE	Anty	8	Ticonderoga	St Louis	14
DOYLE	Bess		Ticonderoga		45
DOYLE	Betty	19	Ticonderoga		
DOYLE	Catherine	28	Ticonderoga		7
DOYLE	Catherine	35	Ticonderoga	St Louis	14
DOYLE	E	30	Loodianah		147
DOYLE	Ellen		Ticonderoga		45
DOYLE	James		Ticonderoga		45
DOYLE	James	3	Ticonderoga	St Louis	14
DOYLE	James	6	Ticonderoga		83
DOYLE	John	22	Loodianah		147
DOYLE	Kate	6	Ticonderoga	St Louis	14
DOYLE	Margaret	22	Ticonderoga		7
DOYLE	Margaret	28	Ticonderoga		83
DOYLE	Mary	28	Ticonderoga		

Surname	First name	Age	Ship	Location	Code
DOYLE	Mary Ann	10	Ticonderoga	St Louis	14
DOYLE	Mary Anne	18	Chasca		
DOYLE	Michael	25	Ticonderoga		45
DOYLE	Michael	4	Ticonderoga		83
DOYLE	P	27	Loodianah		
DOYLE	Patt	21	Ticonderoga		
DOYLE	Patt	22	Ticonderoga		
DOYLE	Peter	13	Ticonderoga	St Louis	14
DOYLE	Sarah		Ticonderoga		45
DOYLE	Terence	22	Ticonderoga		
DOYLE	Terence	30	Ticonderoga		83
DOYLE	Thomas	40	Ticonderoga		45
DOYLE	William	12	Ticonderoga	St Louis	14
DOYLE	William	26	Loodianah		
DOYLE	William	40	Ticonderoga	St Louis	14
DRUM	J	21	Loodianah		
DUNN	Bridget	23	Ticonderoga	St Louis	
DUNNE	Stephen	22	Ticonderoga		
DWYER	Cornelius	25	Chasca		125
DWYER	John	22	Chasca		125
DWYER	Saney	24	Chasca		
ENGLISH	Hetty	19	Ticonderoga		
ESMOND	Sarah	43	Ticonderoga	Wexford	
FARRELL	Peter	46	Ticonderoga		
FARRELL	Thomas	25	Ticonderoga		
FASE	Fanne	20	Chasca		
FENELL	Marget	22	Chasca		124
FENELL	Mary	?	Chasca		124
FENNELL	Mary	22	Ticonderoga	Wexford	
FINN	Daniel	28	Ticonderoga	Wexford	
FITZGERALD	James	3	Ticonderoga		42
FITZGERALD	Maurice		Ticonderoga		42
FITZGERALD	Patrick	8	Ticonderoga		42
FITZGERALD	Sally	30	Ticonderoga		42
FITZGERALD	James	17	Ticonderoga	St Louis	
FITZWILLIAM	Patrick	12	Ticonderoga		
FLAHERTY	Peter	25	Ticonderoga		

Surname	First name	Age	Ship	Location	Code
FLEMING	Ann	22	Chasca		
FLEMING	Ellen	23	Chasca		112
FLEMING	James	30	Chasca		112
FLEMING	Mary	Inf	Chasca		112
FLEMING	Patrick	2	Chasca		112
FLYNNE	Cath	14	Chasca		
FLYNNE	Owen	14	Chasca		
FOGARTY	Ellen	18	Chasca		
FOGARTY	John	28	Chasca		
FOLAN	Bridget	24	Chasca		106
FOLAN	Mary	Inf	Chasca		106
FOLEY	Margaret	27	Ticonderoga		17
FOLEY	Mathew	26	Ticonderoga		
FOLEY	Thomas	30	Ticonderoga		17
FORDE	James	28	Chasca		
FORTESCUE	John	32	Chasca		
FOSSETT	Elis	29	Chasca		
FRALREY	Thos	17	Loodianah		150
FRALEY	Thos	40	Loodianah		150
FRANEY	Bridget	24	Ticonderoga		21
FRANEY	Bridget	55	Ticonderoga		21
FRANEY	Catherine	28	Ticonderoga		21
FRANEY	Joseph	27	Ticonderoga		21
FRANEY	Patrick	5	Ticonderoga		21
FRANEY	Patt	16	Ticonderoga		
FRANEY	Stephen	30	Ticonderoga		21
FRENEY	Peggy		Ticonderoga		
GAFFNEY	Dennis	22	Chasca		
GARDNER	Thom	79?	Chasca		
GARRETY	Mary	25	Chasca		
GESDART	Ludwig	32	Chasca		
GLAYDON	Michael	30	Chasca		
GORMAN	John	19	Ticonderoga	St Louis	
GORTLAND	John	25	Ticonderoga		
GOSLIN	Eliza	7	Ticonderoga		85
GOSLIN	James	30	Ticonderoga		85
GOSLIN	Mary	20	Ticonderoga	St Louis	

Surname	First name	Age	Ship	Location	Code
GOSLIN	Mary	21	Ticonderoga		85
GOSS	P	30	Loodianah		
GOTLAND	John	22	Loodianah		140
GOTLAND	L	24	Loodianah		140
GRADY	T	17	Loodianah		
GRAHAM	Miles	33	Ticonderoga		
GRANEY	Bridget	18	Chasca		
GUESTER	Anna	24	Chasca		
GUILLENONE	Nicola	65	Chasca		
HALL	James	26	Loodianah		
HALLORAN	Catherine	26	Chasca		
HALLORAND	Elizabeth	20	Chasca		
HAMILTON	Dennis	32	Ticonderoga		19
HAMILTON	Ellen	28	Ticonderoga		19
HANLON	Bryan	22	Chasca		
HARNEY	Anne	19	Ticonderoga		61
HARNEY	Arthur	22	Ticonderoga		61
HARNEY	Bessy	17	Ticonderoga		61
HARNEY	John	30	Ticonderoga		61
HARNEY	Mary	24	Ticonderoga		61
HARNEY	Mary	60	Ticonderoga		61
HARNEY	Michael	33	Ticonderoga		61
HARNEY	Philip	28	Ticonderoga		61
HARRINGTON	John	16	Chasca		107
HARRINGTON	Maurice	30	Chasca		
HARRINGTON	Patt	50	Chasca		107
HATCH	John	22	Ticonderoga		
HAYDEN	Mathew	22	Ticonderoga		24
HAYDEN	Thomas	22	Ticonderoga		24
HEALEY	James	20	Ticonderoga		
HEALY	James	30	Loodianah		
HEASE	Cath	20	Chasca		
HEATLEY	Abraham	14	Ticonderoga	Wexford	1
HEATLEY	Christina	16	Ticonderoga	Wexford	1
HEATLEY	Daniel	5	Ticonderoga	Wexford	1
HEATLEY	Edward	7	Ticonderoga	Wexford	1
HEATLEY	Eliza	12	Ticonderoga	Wexford	1

Surname	First name	Age	Ship	Location	Code
HEATLEY	Eliza	40	Ticonderoga	Wexford	1
HEATLEY	Fanny		Ticonderoga	Wexford	1
HEATLEY	Lucy	2	Ticonderoga	Wexford	1
HEATLEY	William	50	Ticonderoga	Wexford	1
HENDER	Thomas	24	Ticonderoga		
HENDRICK	Andrew	23	Ticonderoga	Fort Smith	
HENNEY	P	24	Loodianah		
HEYFRON	Daniel	7	Ticonderoga	Wexford	43
HEYFRON	Esther	25	Ticonderoga	Wexford	43
HEYFRON	Martin	22	Ticonderoga	Wexford	43
HEYFRON	Mary	44	Ticonderoga	Wexford	43
HEYFRON	Mary Anne	8	Ticonderoga	Wexford	43
HEYFRON	Michael	25	Ticonderoga	Wexford	43
HOGAN	Alice	7	Ticonderoga		12
HOGAN	Anne	7	Ticonderoga		12
HOGAN	James	38	Ticonderoga		12
HOGAN	Mary	2	Ticonderoga		12
HOGAN	Mary	35	Ticonderoga		
HOGAN	Mary	38	Ticonderoga		12
HOGAN	William	5	Ticonderoga		12
HOLT	Mary	25	Chasca		122
HOLT	William	26	Chasca		122
HOOLEHAN	Luse	35	Chasca		
HOOTHNER	Jos	25	Chasca		
HOPKINS	Bridget	22	Chasca		
HORAN	?	13	Chasca		131
HORAN	Cath	28	Chasca		131
HORE	Thomas	54	Ticonderoga	Wexford	
HOSSER	Geo	35	Chasca		
HUGHES	Biddy	24	Ticonderoga		
HUGHES	Thomas	32	Loodianah		
HUGHS	Cath	30	Chasca		
HUGO	William	23	Loodianah		
HUNTY	Cath	30	Chasca		116
HUNTY	Daniel	32	Chasca		116
HUNTY	Dennis	6	Chasca		116
HUNTY	Jeremiah	8	Chasca		116

Surname	First name	Age	Ship	Location	Code
HUNTY	Johanna	4	Chasca		116
HUNTY	John	Inf	Chasca		116
INMAN	John	20	Ticonderoga	St Louis	
JACKMAN	Patt	33	Ticonderoga		
JOHNSTON	Ann	12	Chasca		90
JOHNSTON	Mary	40	Chasca		90
KANE	Bridget	18	Chasca		
KANE	Margaret	22	Ticonderoga		26
KANE	Patrick	18	Ticonderoga		26
KANE	Patt	24	Chasca		102
KANE	Richard	20	Chasca		102
KAVANAGH	Anne	17	Ticonderoga		27
KAVANAGH	Biddy	21	Ticonderoga		27
KAVANAGH	Edward	26	Ticonderoga		
KAVANAGH	Laurence	21	Ticonderoga		
KAVANAGH	Mary	25	Ticonderoga		
KAVANAGH	Peter	26	Ticonderoga		
KAVANAGH	Richard	22	Ticonderoga		
KAVANAH	Andy	28	Chasca		88
KAVANAH	Ann	4	Chasca		88
KAVANAH	Ellen	Inf	Chasca		88
KAVANAH	Julia	Inf	Chasca		88
KAVANAH	Margaret	25	Chasca		88
KAVANAH	Thomas	30	Chasca		88
KAVANNAH	James	25	Loodianah		
KEATING	Anna	30	Chasca		
KEATING	Anne	6	Ticonderoga	Fort Smith	50
KEATING	James	40	Ticonderoga	Fort Smith	50
KEATING	Laurence	1	Ticonderoga	Fort Smith	50
KEATING	Mary	30	Ticonderoga	Fort Smith	50
KEATING	Mary	8	Ticonderoga	Fort Smith	50
KEATING	Patt	27	Ticonderoga		
KEEFE	?	30	Chasca		130
KEEFE	Bryan	36	Ticonderoga	Fort Smith	64
KEEFE	Honora	2	Chasca		130
KEEFE	John	14	Ticonderoga	Fort Smith	64
KEEFE	Mary	34	Ticonderoga	Fort Smith	64

Surname	First name	Age	Ship	Location	Code
KEEFE	Timothy	40	Chasca		130
KEHOE	James	21	Loodianah		
KEHOE	M	21	Loodianah		
KELLEY	Ellen	55	Chasca		
KELLEY	June	11	Chasca		
KELLEY	Mary	28	Chasca	Died on ship	93
KELLEY	Peter	30	Chasca		93
KELLY	Betty	18	Ticonderoga	Fort Smith	49
KELLY	Biddy	13	Ticonderoga	Fort Smith	49
KELLY	E	1	Loodianah		144
KELLY	George	22	Ticonderoga	Fort Smith	49
KELLY	James	12	Loodianah		144
KELLY	James	26	Ticonderoga	Fort Smith	49
KELLY	John	23	Chasca		
KELLY	John	35	Loodianah		144
KELLY	Mary	51	Ticonderoga	Fort Smith	49
KELLY	Nicholas	20	Ticonderoga	Fort Smith	49
KELLY	Tobias	51	Ticonderoga	Fort Smith	49
KELLY	William	3	Loodianah		144
KENELUM	Mary	21	Chasca		
KENILOUS	J	28	Loodianah		138
KENILOUS	James	18	Loodianah		138
KENILOUS	John (1)	22	Loodianah		138
KENILOUS	John (2)	22	Loodianah		138
KENILOUS	Thomas	28	Loodianah		138
KENILOUS	William	24	Loodianah		138
KENNEDY	John	38	Ticonderoga		
KENNEDY	John	42	Loodianah		
KENNY	Dennis	35	Ticonderoga		36
KENNY	James	27	Loodianah		
KENNY	John	25	Ticonderoga	St Louis	135
KENNY	Julia	23	Ticonderoga	St Louis	135
KENNY	Mary	33	Ticonderoga		36
KENRELL	John	24	Loodianah		
KEOGH	Catherine	30	Ticonderoga		20
KEOGH	Christopher	35	Ticonderoga		20
KEOGH	Ellen	6	Ticonderoga		20

Surname	First name	Age	Ship	Location	Code
KEOGH	John	5	Ticonderoga		20
KEOGH	Mary	12	Ticonderoga		20
KEOGH	Michael	9	Ticonderoga		20
KEOGH	Miles	15	Ticonderoga		20
KEOGH	Miles	23	Ticonderoga		74
KEOGH	Patt	45	Ticonderoga		
KEOGH	Sarah	14	Ticonderoga		20
KEOGH	Sarah	26	Ticonderoga		74
KEOGH	Sarah	60	Ticonderoga		
KEOGH	Thomas	17	Ticonderoga		20
KERWIN	Catherine	18	Ticonderoga		
KERWIN	James	22	Ticonderoga		57
KERWIN	James	60	Ticonderoga		57
KERWIN	John	24	Ticonderoga		57
KERWIN	John	40	Ticonderoga		
KERWIN	Winnefred		Ticonderoga		57
KICKHAM	Thom	30	Chasca		
KINCELLA	Anne	5	Ticonderoga		62
KINCELLA	Arthur	23	Ticonderoga		30
KINCELLA	Betty	25	Ticonderoga		39
KINCELLA	Betty	49	Ticonderoga		62
KINCELLA	Dennis	14	Ticonderoga		62
KINCELLA	Dennis	50	Ticonderoga		62
KINCELLA	Edward	17	Ticonderoga		62
KINCELLA	Edward	26	Ticonderoga		30
KINCELLA	James	20	Ticonderoga		8
KINCELLA	James	24	Ticonderoga		62
KINCELLA	John	18	Ticonderoga		62
KINCELLA	John	40	Ticonderoga		
KINCELLA	Mary	18	Ticonderoga		30
KINCELLA	Mary	7	Ticonderoga		62
KINCELLA	Michael	26	Ticonderoga		
KINCELLA	Michael	27	Ticonderoga		8
KINCELLA	Miles	25	Ticonderoga		39
KINCELLA	Patrick	13	Ticonderoga		62
KOWMAN	Thomas	25	Loodianah		
LACE	Augustus	28	Chasca		

Surname	First name	Age	Ship	Location	Code
LAMB	Peter	28	Chasca		
LAMBERT	Catherine	24	Ticonderoga		73
LAMBERT	Charles	29	Ticonderoga		73
LAMBERT	Esther		Ticonderoga		73
LAMBERT	John	31	Loodianah		
LAMBERT	Mary	24	Ticonderoga		73
LANE	Patt	40	Chasca		
LAWLESS	Catherine	16	Ticonderoga		
LAWLESS	John	24	Loodianah		
LEAHANE	Abigail	30	Chasca		110
LEAHANE	John	35	Chasca		110
LEARY	John	27	Ticonderoga		
LEARY	Michael	20	Chasca		
LEECH	Thomas	17	Ticonderoga		
LINCH	?	35	Chasca		109
LINCH	Betsey	4	Chasca		109
LINCH	Bridget	30	Chasca		109
LINCH	Mary	Inf	Chasca		109
LOFTUS	Patt	26	Chasca		
LOOK	James	22	Loodianah		
LOYD	Cath	22	Chasca		
LYNCH	Mary	15	Chasca		
LYNCH	Thomas J	27	Ticonderoga		
LYNCH	William	22	Chasca		
M'CAREE	Patrick	25	Chasca		
MAGEE	Luke	32	Ticonderoga		
MAHER	Cath	23	Chasca		
MALEASEY	Cath	20	Chasca		
MALONY	Margaret	25	Chasca		
MARTIN	Patrick		Ticonderoga	Little Rock	
McANEELEY	John	24	Chasca		
McCANN	Patt	25	Ticonderoga	St Louis	
McCANNON	James	15	Chasca		
McCUE	Margaret	23	Chasca		
McDONALD	Hugh	30	Ticonderoga		
McDONNELL	Bess	16	Ticonderoga		76
McDONNELL	John	20	Ticonderoga		76

Surname	First name	Age	Ship	Location	Code
McDONNELL	Maria	7	Ticonderoga		76
McDONNELL	Mary	36	Ticonderoga		76
McDONNELL	Mathew	14	Ticonderoga		76
McDONNELL	Patt	47	Ticonderoga		76
McDONNELL	Philip	20	Ticonderoga	St Louis	
McDONNELL	Thomas		Ticonderoga		76
McMAHON	Patt	13	Chasca		
McMAHON	Ross	17	Chasca		
McMANUS	Thomas	16	Ticonderoga		
McQUINN	Michael	26	Chasca		129
McQUINN	Michael	4	Chasca		129
McQUIRK	Biddy	23	Ticonderoga		
MIDDLETON	Bridget	35	Chasca		
MONAHAN	Mary	30	Chasca		108
MONAHAN	Winafred	4	Chasca		108
MOORE	Margaret	19	Ticonderoga	St Louis	
MORAN	Edward	15	Chasca		100
MORAN	Winnefred	26	Chasca		100
MORRIS	Eliza	24	Ticonderoga	St Louis	
MORRISSEY	Edward	22	Chasca		
MULHALL	Joseph	34	Ticonderoga		70
MULHALL	Judy		Ticonderoga		70
MULHALL	L	30	Loodianah		
MULHALL	Mary	50	Ticonderoga		59
MULHALL	Miles	20	Ticonderoga		
MULHALL	P	13	Loodianah		
MULHALL	William	55	Ticonderoga		59
MULLAGEN	Anne	20	Chasca		118
MULLAGEN	Edward	Inf	Chasca		118
MULLAGEN	John	30	Chasca		118
MULLAGEN	Widow	50	Chasca		118
MULLEN	John	25	Chasca		
MULLEN	Martin	20	Ticonderoga		
MULLEN	Mary	40	Chasca		
MULLER	Edward	27	Chasca		
MULLIGAN	P	22	Loodianah		
MUNSOW	John	28	Chasca		

Surname	First name	Age	Ship	Location	Code
MUR	Ernest	23	Chasca		
MURNA	James	28	Ticonderoga		52
MURNA	Mary	26	Ticonderoga		52
MURNA	Owen	24	Ticonderoga		
MURPHY	Andy	28	Ticonderoga		47
MURPHY	Anne	2	Ticonderoga		47
MURPHY	Anne	22	Ticonderoga		23
MURPHY	Anne	40	Ticonderoga	St Louis	78
MURPHY	Betty	14	Ticonderoga	St Louis	60
MURPHY	Betty	25	Ticonderoga		23
MURPHY	Betty	27	Ticonderoga		47
MURPHY	Biddy	35	Ticonderoga		53
MURPHY	Bridget	13	Ticonderoga	St Louis	78
MURPHY	Catherine	12	Ticonderoga	St Louis	60
MURPHY	Catherine	50	Ticonderoga	St Louis	60
MURPHY	Dennis	13	Chasca		94
MURPHY	Dennis	42	Ticonderoga	St Louis	78
MURPHY	Dennis	8	Ticonderoga	St Louis	78
MURPHY	Edmond	14	Ticonderoga		
MURPHY	Edward	11	Ticonderoga	St Louis	78
MURPHY	Ellen	15	Ticonderoga	St Louis	78
MURPHY	Ellen	17	Ticonderoga	St Louis	60
MURPHY	Ellen	30	Chasca		
MURPHY	Frances	21	Chasca		
MURPHY	Francis	14	Ticonderoga		53
MURPHY	Frank	26	Ticonderoga	Wexford	9
MURPHY	George	22	Ticonderoga	Wexford	9
MURPHY	George	40	Ticonderoga		53
MURPHY	George	6	Ticonderoga		53
MURPHY	James	11	Ticonderoga		53
MURPHY	James	19	Ticonderoga	St Louis	60
MURPHY	John	55	Ticonderoga	St Louis	60
MURPHY	John	6	Ticonderoga	St Louis	78
MURPHY	John	60	Chasca		94
MURPHY	Jonathan	16	Ticonderoga	St Louis	78
MURPHY	M	26	Loodianah		
MURPHY	Martin	22	Chasca		95

Surname	First name	Age	Ship	Location	Code
MURPHY	Martin	23	Chasca		94
MURPHY	Mary	22	Chasca		94
MURPHY	Mary	22	Ticonderoga	St Louis	60
MURPHY	Mary	24	Ticonderoga		
MURPHY	Mary	25	Chasca		119
MURPHY	Mary	9	Ticonderoga	St Louis	78
MURPHY	Michael	50	Ticonderoga	St Louis	60
MURPHY	P	30	Loodianah		
MURPHY	Patrick	26	Chasca		26
MURPHY	Paul	30	Ticonderoga		
MURPHY	Stephen	26	Chasca		119
NEAL	Arthur	23	Ticonderoga		
NEAL	Catherine	19	Ticonderoga		
NEAL	Daniel	26	Ticonderoga		2
NEAL	Fanny	24	Ticonderoga		2
NEAL	John	33	Chasca		
NEAL	Laurence	26	Ticonderoga		
NEAL	Laurence	26	Ticonderoga		66
NEAL	Margaret	26	Ticonderoga		66
NEALE	B	25	Loodianah		
NEALE	Charles	18	Ticonderoga		81
NEALE	Dolly		Ticonderoga		81
NEALE	James	22	Ticonderoga		
NEIL	Henry	27	Ticonderoga		
NEIL	Margaret	19	Ticonderoga		
NEIL	Thomas	26	Loodianah		
NICKELSON	Robert	21	Chasca		
NOBLE	Anne	26	Chasca		
NOBLE	Bess	28	Chasca		114
NOBLE	Jarrat	30	Chasca		114
NOLAN	Andrew	20	Ticonderoga	Wexford	
NOLAN	Eliza	19	Ticonderoga		
NOOLAN	P	20	Loodianah		
NOWLAN	Anne	30	Ticonderoga		
NOWLAN	Catherine	22	Ticonderoga		75
NOWLAN	Catherine	7	Ticonderoga		56
NOWLAN	Daniel	54	Ticonderoga		56

Surname	First name	Age	Ship	Location	Code
NOWLAN	Darby	30	Ticonderoga		35
NOWLAN	Dennis	13	Ticonderoga		56
NOWLAN	Eliza	10	Ticonderoga		35
NOWLAN	James	15	Ticonderoga		56
NOWLAN	John	17	Ticonderoga		56
NOWLAN	Martin	20	Ticonderoga		56
NOWLAN	Mary	20	Ticonderoga		75
NOWLAN	Mary	23	Ticonderoga		35
NOWLAN	Mary	3	Ticonderoga		35
NOWLAN	Mary	9	Ticonderoga		56
NOWLAN	Peter	5	Ticonderoga		56
NOWLAN	Sally	45	Ticonderoga		56
NOWLAN	Thomas	22	Ticonderoga		56
NOWLAND	Martha	21	Chasca		103
NOWLAND	Richard	16	Chasca		103
NOWLAND	William	18	Chasca		103
O'BRIEN	A	27	Loodianah		
O'FARRELL	J	26	Loodianah		
O'HARA	Neel	20	Ticonderoga		
O'LEARY	Catherine	25	Chasca		
ORMOND	Catherine	20	Ticonderoga		
PACEY	John	22	Loodianah		
PAYNE	Thos	18	Chasca		
POINDABLE	Michael	20	Chasca		
PUGH	Betty	25	Ticonderoga		44
PUGH	Betty	4	Ticonderoga		44
PUGH	Henry	3	Ticonderoga		44
PUGH	James	35	Ticonderoga		44
PUGH	James	5	Ticonderoga		44
PUGH	John	7	Ticonderoga		44
QUIGLEY	Bridget	22	Chasca		
QUIGLEY	James	49	Chasca		
RAFFERTY	William	20	Chasca		
RAWLEY	Catherine	3	Chasca		105
RAWLEY	James	28	Chasca		105
RAWLEY	Johanna	Inf	Chasca		105
RAWLEY	Margaret	28	Chasca		105

Surname	First name	Age	Ship	Location	Code
RAWLEY	Michael	4	Chasca		105
REDMOND	Alice	45	Ticonderoga		79
REDMOND	Charles	30	Ticonderoga		
REDMOND	Edward	17	Ticonderoga		79
REDMOND	Edward	25	Ticonderoga		
REDMOND	Eliza	6	Ticonderoga		79
REDMOND	Ellen	20	Ticonderoga		28
REDMOND	Garret	30	Chasca		92
REDMOND	Henry	14	Ticonderoga	St Louis	28
REDMOND	James	25	Ticonderoga		
REDMOND	James	26	Ticonderoga		28
REDMOND	James	53	Ticonderoga		28
REDMOND	Kate		Ticonderoga		28
REDMOND	Margaret	20	Ticonderoga		
REDMOND	Margaret	8	Ticonderoga		79
REDMOND	Martha	25	Ticonderoga		28
REDMOND	Mary	18	Ticonderoga		28
REDMOND	Mary	28	Chasca		92
REDMOND	Mary	50	Ticonderoga		28
REDMOND	Patrick	19	Ticonderoga		79
REDMOND	Sally	10	Ticonderoga		79
REDMOND	Thomas	30	Chasca		
REDMOND	William	25	Ticonderoga		
REILLY	James	18	Ticonderoga	St Louis	65
REILLY	Patrick	35	Ticonderoga	Little Rock	
REILLY	Thomas	22	Ticonderoga		65
REYNOLDS	Andy	28	Chasca		96
REYNOLDS	Betty	25	Chasca		96
REYNOLDS	Ellen	13	Chasca		96
REYNOLDS	Patrick	26	Chasca		96
REYNOLDS	Stephen	39	Chasca		96
RIDLEY	Lawrence	19	Chasca		
ROCHE	Florence	20	Chasca		
ROGAN	Catherine	24	Ticonderoga		71
ROGAN	Hugh	28	Ticonderoga		71
ROURK	L	20	Loodianah		
ROURKE	Bridget	19	Ticonderoga		10

Surname	First name	Age	Ship	Location	Code
ROURKE	Catherine	22	Ticonderoga		5
ROURKE	Catherine	23	Ticonderoga		10
ROURKE	Martin	25	Ticonderoga		5
RUN	Caroline	21	Chasca		132
RUN	Charles	45	Chasca		132
RUSH	Bridget	20	Chasca		91
RUSH	John	22	Chasca		
RUSH	Margaret	18	Chasca		91
RUSH	Peter	25	Chasca		91
RUSSELL	Cath	30	Chasca		
RYAN	Eliza	20	Ticonderoga	St Louis	
RYAN	James	21	Chasca		
RYAN	John	18	Loodianah		
RYAN	John	30	Loodianah		
RYAN	Mary	18	Ticonderoga	St Louis	4
RYAN	Owen	16	Ticonderoga	St Louis	4
RYAN	Thomas	20	Ticonderoga	St Louis	4
SCALLION	Catherine	23	Ticonderoga		11
SCALLION	James	29	Ticonderoga		11
SENNETT	Andrew	26	Ticonderoga		
SHANAHAN	Patt	28	Chasca		
SHEA	Patt	34	Ticonderoga		
SHEAN	John	22	Chasca		126
SHEAN	Mary	20	Chasca		126
SHEAN	Michael	26	Chasca		126
SHERIDAN	Margaret	26	Ticonderoga		
SHOENAN	Albert	26	Chasca		
SINNETT	Anne	11	Chasca		
SINNOTT	Catherine	21	Ticonderoga		
SINNOTT	Thomas	22	Ticonderoga		
SMITH	Margaret	Inf	Chasca		113
SMITH	Mary	26	Chasca		113
SOMERS	Elizabeth	15	Ticonderoga		37
SOMERS	Timothy	15	Ticonderoga		37
SOUTH	Thos	27	Loodianah		
SPENCER	Charles	20	Ticonderoga		
St. LEDGER	Peter	34	Ticonderoga		

Surname	First name	Age	Ship	Location	Code
STAFFORD	Edmund	35	Ticonderoga	Wexford	
STANTON	Bridget	35	Chasca		
STANTON	William	23	Ticonderoga		
SULIVAN	Bridget	40	Chasca		
SULLIVAN	Cath	24	Chasca		128
SULLIVAN	Dennis	35	Chasca		
SULLIVAN	James	23	Chasca		128
SULLIVAN	Patt	26	Chasca		
SUMMERS	John	26	Loodianah		
SUNDERLAN	J	25	Loodianah		
THEOGH	M	30	Loodianah		145
THEOGH	P	25	Loodianah		145
TIMMONS	Mary	26	Ticonderoga		
TOBIN	Bridget	21	Chasca		
TOBIN	Patrick	25	Chasca		
TOBIN	Patt	24	Chasca		
TOOLE	Anne	28	Ticonderoga		25
TOOLE	Catherine	55	Ticonderoga		33
TOOLE	James	24	Ticonderoga		25
TOOLE	John	25	Ticonderoga		
TOOLE	John	26	Ticonderoga		25
TOOLE	John	34	Loodianah		
TOOLE	Margaret	20	Ticonderoga		33
TOOLE	Mary	20	Ticonderoga		
TOOLE	Mary	22	Ticonderoga		33
TOOLE	Owen	25	Ticonderoga		
TOOLE	Rich'd	24	Chasca		
TOOLE	William	24	Ticonderoga		33
TRAVERS	Peter	22	Ticonderoga		
TRAYNOR	P	20	Loodianah		
TUITE	Thomas	30	Ticonderoga		
TULLY	Andrew	20	Chasca		121
TULLY	Catherine	50	Chasca		121
TULLY	James	24	Chasca		121
TULLY	John	36	Chasca		121
TULLY	Mary	21	Chasca		121
TUOE	John	8	Chasca		

Surname	First name	Age	Ship	Location	Code
TUTTY	James	24	Ticonderoga		
TWOMEY	Daniel	23	Chasca		
TWOMEY	John	30	Loodianah		
VAUGHAN	Charles	20	C		
WAFER	Michael	24	Chasca		
WALSH	Ann	20	Ticonderoga	St Louis	
WALSH	Cath	22	Chasca		
WALSH	J	20	Loodianah		
WARD	D	19	Loodianah		137
WARD	John	55	Loodianah		
WARD	L	13	Loodianah		
WARD	N	13	Loodianah		137
WARE	L	50	Loodianah		141
WARE	P	26	Loodianah		141
WARE	P	50	Loodianah		141
WELDON	Darby	35	Chasca		98
WELDON	Peggy	28	Chasca		98
WERN	J	21	Loodianah		148
WERN	James	47	Loodianah		148
WHELAN	Esther		Ticonderoga		
WHELAN	James	26	Loodianah		139
WHELAN	John	21	Ticonderoga		77
WHELAN	Mary	19	Ticonderoga		77
WHELAN	Peggy	30	Ticonderoga		
WHELAN	Sarah	21	Ticonderoga		
WHELAN	Thomas	23	Ticonderoga		
WHELAN	William	23	Loodianah		139
WHITE	Arthur	30	Chasca		
WHITE	James	25	Loodianah		
WHITE	Patt	20	Chasca		127
WHITE	William	17	Chasca		127
WHITLES	Anne	28	Chasca		
WOLFE	John	21	Chasca		
WOODS	John	45	Loodianah		
WOODS	P	30	Loodianah		

Chronology

1698   Introduction of the Penal Laws which greatly denied civil liberties to all except members of the Established Church. The most successful of these measures were those designed to transfer landownership from Catholics to Protestants.

1790s   An estimated 5% of land remained in Catholic ownership.

1796 c   Birth of Thomas Hore, Coldblow, County Wexford.

1798   Armed rebellion against the British rule in Ireland.

1801   The Act of Union by which Britain once more took direct control of all Irish affairs, both internal and external

1814 c   Thomas Hore entered St Kieran's College to study for the priesthood.

1820   Hore arrived in Richmond, Virginia with his mentor, Dr Kelly, who had been appointed bishop to the new see. Hore ordained in Richmond.

1821   Kelly returned to Ireland. A successor was not appointed until 1841 – twenty years later.

1827   Overwork takes its toll and Hore returns to the diocese of Ferns in Ireland.

1827-41   Thomas Hore was pastor in the mensal parish of Camolin, County Wexford.

1841   Thomas Hore became parish priest of the combined parishes of Killaveny and Annacurra in Co Wicklow.
–Irish population at all-time high, having doubled to over eight million in forty years.

1843   Andrew Byrne became bishop of Little Rock, Arkansas.

1844   Bishop Byrne builds small church in Little Rock.

1845   The potato crop failed in Ireland.

1846-47   The worst period of the Great Famine.

1848   Abbot of Mount Melleray, County Waterford, planned on establishing a new house in America.
— Young Ireland Rebellion.
— Effects of the Famine worsened with each passing week.
— Emigration at all-time high.
— Bishop Byrne consecrated new church in Fort Smith and set his plan in motion to establish one or two Irish colonies in his Little Rock diocese.

1849   Work on New Melleray in Iowa began. Plans to attract Irish colonists to that part of the U.S. frontier also well advanced.

April 12th, 1850	Fr Francis Walsh arrived in Iowa from Waterford as prior to the new house.
June 2nd, 1850	Fr Hore gave his last sermon in Ireland, calling on as many families as possible to accompany him to America.
June 3rd, 1850	Royal Irish Constabulary Report on the above sermon filed.
June – Sept 1850	Getting in names of all those intending to travel to the United States.
October 1850	Emigrants arrive in Liverpool. First contingent reported being there by the 19th.
October 22nd, 1850	Fr Hore met Bishop Byrne in Liverpool and was appointed vicar-general of the diocese of Little Rock with specific responsibility of getting the group to Arkansas.
October 24th, 1850	Both 'Ticonderoga' and 'Loodianah' cleared Liverpool
November 2nd, 1850	'Chasca' followed.
December 3rd, 1850	'Ticonderoga' arrived at New Orleans.
December 20th, 1850	'Loodianah' arrived at New Orleans.
December 20th, 1850	Arkansas Gazette stated that 'about 100' of the expected immigrants had arrived in excellent health and urged the community to welcome them with open arms and open doors.

Dec 1850 – Jan 51	A cholera-like desease erupted among the group eventually killing an estimated twenty of them.
Jan 51	Hore and small group left Little Rock for Fort Smith. The bulk of the others went to St Louis.
January 3rd or 11th, 1851	'Chasca' reaches New Orleans
January 23rd, 1851	Fr Hore reached Dubuque, Iowa
February 4th, 1851	Bishop Byrne and Sisters of Mercy arrived in Little Rock on board the steamboat 'Pontiac' to find that most of Hore's group had gone to St Louis and that he was following them after he had settled some families in Fort Smith.
February 14th, 1851	Open attack on Bishop Byrne and the Sisters of Mercy by the Arkansas Gazette for the way the sick and dying had been 'deserted'.
February 22nd, 1851	Hore purchased over 1,000 acres of land at $1.25 an acre in Lafayette and Taylor townships in Iowa.
February 24th, 1851	Hore purchased a further 700 acres in the same area at the same price.
March 17th, 1851	Three seminarians who travelled on the 'Ticonderoga' ordained in Little Rock.
-	Bishop Byrne established the Hibernian Benevolent Society in that city.
March 1851	Hore returned to St Louis to bring his followers to Iowa.
March 25th, 1851	Hore and only eighteen families arrived at Lafayette Landing.
April 16th, 1851	Hore made final purchase of 320 acres.
-	Hore loaned $490 to New Melleray
April 23rd, 1851	Church at Wexford, Iowa completed.
May 25th, 1851	New Melleray repaid the loan of April 16th.
July 8th, 1852	Hore deeded 520 acres of land to F.Welch, T.C.Smith, A.L.Byrne for $1,600. These three purchasers were members of the New

	Melleray Community and no money changed hands.
6th December, 1852	Fr Walsh resigned as prior of New Melleray. His successor was Fr C Smyth.
August 30th, 1853	Prior Smyth went to Wexford, Iowa.
September 8th, 1852	Day before Prior Smyth returned to New Melleray, the same property deeded on July 8th, 1852 was made over to Timothy C. Smyth, Francis Walsh, and Ambrose L Byrne for the sum of $1.
June 11th, 1855	Prior Smyth and another monk spent some time in Wexford, probably finalising plans for a new monastery to be built there.
June 18th, 1855	Hore deed another 320 acres to 'Byrnes, Ambrose L; T.C.Smyth; and Fr Walsh' for the sum of $900. Again this was purely a paper transaction.
June 22nd, 1855	Smyth and the other monk return to New Melleray.
April 11th, 1857	Dom James O'Gorman succeeded Smyth as prior of New Melleray.
May 1857	Hore deeded over the rest of his property to New Melleray.
June 3rd, 1857	Work began on a new monastery at Wexford. Fr Walsh was in charge.
1857	Hore returned to Ireland, then in his early sixties.
June 14th, 1864	Fr Thomas Hore died aged 68.

Notes

Chapter One: The Shaping of Thomas Hore

(1) Schmitz, Kenneth P.: "Father Thomas Hore and Wexford, Iowa"; 'The Past', Journal of the Cumann Seanchais Uí Chinsealaigh; No. 11, 1975-'76. P 3.
(2) Murphy, Hilary; "Families of Co. Wexford"; pp 126-131.
(3) Dolan, T.P & O Muirithe, Diarmaid: "The Past", vol XIII, 1979
(4) Schmitz, op.cit
(5) ibid
(6) ibid
(7) Bailey, James Henry II; "History of St Peter's Church, Richmond, Virginia"; p 11
(8) ibid
(9) Grattan-Flood, W: "History of the Diocese of Ferns"; P 63.
(10) ibid

Chapter Two: The Coolattin Estate

(1) Burke's Peerage, London 1921
(2) Pakenham, Thomas; "The Year of Liberty"
(3) Bence-Jones, Mark (ed): "Burke's Guide to Country Houses" vol 1 Ireland. p 91
(4) Grattan-Flood, W: "History of the Diocese of Ferns". p 63
(5) Lewis's Topographical Dictionary 1837.
(6) "Freeman's Journal", May 10th, 1841
(7) Absentee landlords were so-called because they left their estates in the hands of agents who handled all the business of the estate, while they lived the good life in the parlours and pleasure houses of fashionable London. They neither knew nor cared how their Irish estates were managed. What was important was that the rents were paid and they were able to continue a life of self-indulgence. Absentee-landlordism was the bane of Irish rural society and the cause of many of its ills. Many such landlords never visited their Irish estates even once in their profligate lives.
(8) Fitzwilliam Papers, ms 3987
(9) O'Connell, Maurice R. (ed): "The Correspondence of Daniel O'Connell". In November 1830, Daniel O'Connell was investigating the extent of evictions, both in progress and planned, on the Coolattin estate.

(10) Fitzwilliam Papers, mss 4974 & 4975
(11) As quoted in "The Great Hunger" p 87
(12) "Freeman's Journal" 29th June, 1850

Chapter Three: Disaster

(1)   Woodham-Smith, Cecil; "The Great Hunger". p 30
(2)   Young, Arthur; "Tour in Ireland", as quoted in "The Great Hunger"
(3)   Woodham-Smith; op.cit. p 34
(4)   ibid. p 38
(5)   ibid. p 39
(6)   Hannigan, Ken; "Wicklow in the Famine Years", Wicklow Historical Society Journal 1992
(7)   1841 Census
(8)   Hannigan, Ken; op.cit
(9)   Rev. John McGowan, C.M.: "The Irish Famine of 1847"; Sister M. Assisi (ed): Sisters of the Holy Faith; Dublin 1967, pp 32-39.
(10) Hannigan, Ken; op.cit
(11) Fitzwilliam Papers; A letter from Robert Chaloner to Hore, dated 23 May, 1847, shows Hore's active role in the relief work. ms 3987
(12) Letter from Ken Hannigan to the author 8th December, 1992 referring to notes he had made from the Poor Law Commission Reports
(13) ibid
(14) see note 11 above
(15) Neill, Kenneth: "An Illustrated History of the Irish People"
(16) Fitzwilliam Papers, ms 4974/5
(17) "Independent" (Wexford) 1st June, 1850. The explanation of currency exchange is worth including here. "Multiply the amount of sterling pounds by forty, double the number of shillings and pence which add, divide the product by nine and you have the amount required. Should there be a remainder, each unit is sixpence sterling or eleven cents which also add."

Chapter Four: Bishop Byrne of Arkansas

(1)   Gately, Sr. M.J.; "The Sisters of Mercy"; New York 1931. Also see the booklet celebrating the Diamond Jubilee (1899 – 1974) of the Church of the Immaculate Conception, Fort Smith, Arkansas.
(2)   This name appears as O'Donoghue, Donoghue and Donohue in various subsequent accounts. The confusion over his christian name is more serious in that in some sources it is James (Jubilee booklet from Fort Smith) while in others it is Francis ("Arkansas Frontiers of Mercy").
(3)   The Sisters of Mercy with Jane Ramos: "Arkansas Frontiers of Mercy"; St Edward Press, Fort Smith, 1989. p 9
(4)   Gately: "The Sisters of Mercy". p 272
(5)   Unidentified account of a citizen of Fort Smith recalling his life in the town. He first arrived in Fort Smith in March 1866.
(6)   Gately: "The Sisters of Mercy". p 273

(7)	The Sisters of Mercy: "Arkansas Frontiers of Mercy". p 13
(8)	Jubilee booklet of the Church of the Immaculate Conception
(9)	This is an estimated date, arrived at from a study of known dates of departure, etc.
(10)	I have been unable to ascertain when Bishop Byrne and Fr Hore first communicated with each other, but a great deal of planning had to have taken place between the two men for so large an emigration to Little Rock to take place.
(11)	See p87 for account of Fr O'Donoghue's death
(12)	The Sisters of Mercy: "Arkansas Frontiers of Mercy". p 70

Chapter Five: The Melleray Connection

The outline history of the order in this chapter is based on an article published in "An Sleibhteanach", Irishleabhar, Cholaiste Chnuic Mhelleri", Samhain 1902.

(1)	Cullen papers, letter from Archbishop Cullen to the Propaganda in Rome dated 5th April 1851
(2)	ibid
(3)	Cullen papers 39/2/28. Letter dated 6th May 1851.
(4)	One of the four provinces of Ireland. Wicklow and Wexford are two of the twelve Leinster counties.
(5)	Nativism is discussed elsewhere in the book
(6)	"Freeman's Journal", March 16th, 1850, as quoted by Sr Mary Kelly in "Catholic Immigrant Colonization Projects in the United States, 1815-1860"; U.S.Catholic Historical Society, New York, 1939
(7)	Kelly, Sr Mary, O.P.: "Catholic Immigration Projects in the United States, 1815-1860"; p 177-8
(8)	Schmitz, Kenneth: "The Past".

Chapter Six: Farewell to Famine

(1)	Royal Irish Constabulary records, National Archives.
(2)	Outrage Reports, 1850, 32/105. National Archives. I am deeply indebted to Ken Hannigan of the National Archives for bringing this paper to my attention.
(3)	The church stands in Killaveny townland while on the opposite side of the narrow road which passes it is the townland of Whitefield.
(4)	In predecimal currency the pound was divided into twenty shillings, which were subdivided into twelve pennies. There were, therefore, 240 pennies in the pound. Ten shillings was half a pound or 50p in decimal currency.
(5)	Lynch might have misheard and confused Ohio with Iowa. This means, of course, that Fr Hore must have mentioned Iowa in his address to the congregation which indicates that he was already thinking of Iowa as a possible destination as well as Arkansas. This is the only reference I have found to Ohio.

(6)   Fitzwilliam Papers, mss 4974/5
(7)   Coleman, Terry; "Passage to America", p 24
(8)   Comparison of advertisements in contemporary newspapers show that
       £3-5-0 was the usual fare.
(9)   "Illustrated London News", 19th October, 1850
(10)   "Passenger List of the Ticonderoga, 1850"; The Past Vol XII, 1978,
       Footnotes, p 52
(11)   Sisters of Mercy with Jane Ramos: "Frontiers of Mercy", p 71
(12)   Schmitz, Kenneth: "The Past", vol XI, p5
(13)   Most sources agree on this figure
(14)   Coleman, op.cit. p90
(15)   Copies of letters from Sr. Frances Mary of the Purification (Frances
       Breen's professed name) now in the possession of the Hendricks family,
       Fort Smith.
(16)   Schmitz: op.cit
(17)   Coleman: op.cit. p 67. See also "B&I Line", p 77
(18)   "The Times", 8th December, 1848
(19)   Neal, Frank: "Sectarian Violence, the Liverpool Experience", pp 83/84

Chapter Seven: Liverpool – the Emigrants' Limbo

(1)   Merseyside Maritime Museum, Development of the Port display
(2)   Jackson, Gordon: "The History of Ports", p 75
(3)   Shea, Michael: "Maritime England", p 75
(4)   Merseyside Maritime Museum, Dev. of Port display
(5)   Shea, Michael: op. cit. p 75
(6)   Coleman, Terry: "Passage to America", p 73
(7)   ibid, p.74
(8)   ibid, p.91
(9)   "Liverpool Mercury", 27th September, 1850
(10)   Almost all local and national newspapers of the time gave wide and
       prolonged covereage to this issue. There can be little doubt that the
       coverage and the tone added to the anti-Catholic and anti-Irish (and,
       therefore anti-emigrant) stance of all classes of Liverpudlians.
(11)   Coleman, Terry: op.cit. p 90
(12)   "Liverpool Times", 31th October 1850. This report was also carried by
       the "Independent" (Wexford), on 6th November,1850.
(13)   "Liverpool Times", 7th November, 1850, letter from Andrew O'Brien,
       82 Porter Street to the editor. This address in the Scotland district of the
       city was owned by O'Brien and was known as 'The Beer House' and it
       was described in the 1851 census as a Boarding House most of whose
       residents were Irish en route to America. The Scotland district had the
       highest concentration of Irish people in the city.
(14)   ibid
(15)   Schmitz, Kenneth: "The Past", 1975/6
(16)   According to the "Illustrated London News" of 19th October 1850, the
       first detachment of the group were in the city at that date.

(17)   Schmitz: op.cit
(18)   "Liverpool Telegraph and Shipping Gazette". Various October issues.
(19)   Coleman: op.cit. p 94
(20)   "Illustrated London News", 19th October, 1850
(21)   "Liverpool Telegraph and Shipping Gazette"
(22)   See Appendix 2 for the passenger lists.
(23)   "Liverpool Telegraph and Shipping Gazette".

Chapter Eight: "Water, water everywhere..."

(1)   I am deeply indebted to Francis P. Murphy of Hoylake, Merseyside for all this information about these ships. He found the details in the Customs Bills of Entry in the William Brown Library, Liverpool
(2)   Schmitz, Kenneth: "The Past" 1975/6
(3)   Coleman, Terry: "Passage to America", p 349
(4)   A reconstruction of an emigrant ship's steerage accommodation from this period forms part of the Emigrant Exhibition in the Merseyside Maritime Museum.
(5)   Coleman: op.cit. p 134
(6)   Schmitz: op.cit
(7)   ibid
(8)   Coleman: op.cit. p 124
(9)   'Chasca' Passenger List and Report
(10) "Liverpool Telegraph and Shipping Gazette", 30th December, 1850
(11) There are several discrepancies in the various newspapers and documents with regard to departure and arrival dates of these ships. January 11th is the date quoted in Lloyd's register of February 11th, 1851. However, according to the Passenger Report and List which was signed by Captain Wise and given to the Collector of the District of New Orleans, the date of arrival was January 3rd. In deference to Lloyd's reputation for accuracy, I have opted for January 11th, but that does not explain how Captain Wise signed the Report and List eight days earlier. In any event, these voyages were far from fast. The record for the fastest passage on the Liverpool/New Orleans route was 26 days which was set in 1824. This has been disputed because of the lack of documentary evidence. The fastest irrefutable voyage was made by the 1146 ton 'Wm. Stetson' which left Liverpool on December 23rd, 1853 and arrived in New Orleans on the 24th January, 1854, a total 30 sailing days.
(12) Lloyd's List, 23rd January, 1851

Chapter Nine: New Orleans to Little Rock

(1)   Letter from Sr Frances to the Hendricks family, Fort Smith, stating that the Lynch family had arrived safely back in Ireland. The exact date of the letter is not known but it was sometime in 1862.
(2)   Stickler, Bud: "The Wexford Church"; 'The Iowan' – Iowa's Own Magazine; June/July 1957: p 19. Also mentioned by John P. Byrne, guest

speaker at the 100th anniversary of the Wexford parish in 1948, as reported in the 'Journal' (Lansing, Iowa), 21 July, 1948. For the background to these earlier Refugio settlers from Ireland see Appendix 1.

(3)   Oral tradition among the descendants of those people who carried on to Iowa testify to this. There is reference to this group at the back of the church in Wexford, Iowa.

(4)   I am grateful to Maxine Reilly of the Refugio County museum for showing me a copy of a diary written by one of the 1830s Irish group. In the entries for 1851 she mentioned the arrival of a German group into the area. If an Irish group had arrived there in or about the same time, or even a few years later, wouldn't the writer of the diary have recorded such a momentous occasion? The absence of any such reference must indicate that no Irish group arrived there in the early 1850s. What might have happened to them is open to speculation ranging from drowning in the Gulf of Mexico to stopping off at any point along the route.

(5)   John Byrne talk in 1948

(6)   These ships did not arrive in the port until December 20th and January 11th (or 3rd) respectively. When Fr Hore was already in Little Rock, the 'Loodianah was just completing her voyage and the 'Chasca' was putting into the Virgin Islands.

(7)   Letter from Fr John Finn, historian of the Irish in New Orleans, to the author. 20th April 1993.

(8)   Ibid. At this time, slaves were paid a nominal wage of a dollar-a-day. The result of the Irish poor being prepared to work for less was a series of riots involving the slaves, their owners and the general workforce.

(9)   Niehaus, Earl F, S.M.: "The Irish in New Orleans": A history of St Patrick's parish, New Orleans 1833-1958.

(10)   Coleman, Terry: "Passage to America"; p 196.

(11)   Twain, Mark: "Life on the Mississippi", "Huckleberry Finn"; etc.

(12)   Frontier Restoration Project, Little Rock.

(13)   The Sisters of Mercy with Jane Ramos: "Arkansas Frontiers of Mercy"; pp 70-71

(14)   This figure of 300 appears in most accounts of the group's arrival at Little Rock. The "Arkansas Gazette" claimed that only about one hundred people arrived with Hore at Little Rock.

(15)   "Arkansas Gazette", 20th December, 1850

(16)   The Sisters of Mercy with Jane Ramos: op.cit. p72

(17)   "Arkansas Whig" 3rd July 1851 as quoted in Arkansas Historical Quarterly (undated); "Bypaths of Arkansas History". pp 207-208

(18)   Schmitz, Kenneth P: "Father Thomas Hore and Wexford, Iowa"; 'The Past', p 5 – quoting "Irish Catholic Directory 1865".

(19)   ibid. quoting "The Boston Pilot", Mar.8, (no year) p6

(20)   "Arkansas Gazette", 7th February, 1851

(21)   The "Arkansas Banner" was another Little Rock newspaper. Unfortunately, the issue referred to by the "Gazette" is missing from the collection in the History Commission, Little Rock; University of Texas; and the Library of Congress listings.

(22) "Arkansas Gazette", 14th February, 1851

(23) "Arkansas Whig", 3rd July, 1851 as quoted in footnote 17 above.

Chapter Ten: Fort Smith

(1) Carroll, Mother Austin: "Leaves from the Annals of the Sisters of Mercy", Catholic Publication Society; New York, 1889: Vol 3, p354

(2) "All Hallows Pioneer Priests in the United States: 150th anniversary, 1842-1992"

(3) Guy, Francis Joseph: "The Catholic Church in Arkansas 1541-1843. A Dissertation"; Catholic University of America; 1932

(4) This is the number of families usually quoted and accepted as correct in the Fort Smith area.

(5) Martin, Amelia: "MIGRATION. Ireland-Fort Smith and Points West". Fort Smith Historical Society Journal, 1978. In an article about Tobias Kelly in the same publication, N. J. Kelly also states that the leg of the journey from Little Rock to Fort Smith was by covered wagon.

(6) "Fort Smith Herald", 3rd January, 1851

(7) Patton, J.Fred: "History of Fort Smith": pp 1-5

(8) Gately, Sr M J: "The Sisters of Mercy"; p 273

(9) Martin, Amelia. op.cit

(10) When Byrne's successor, Bishop Fitzgerald, was in a position to repay the loan some years later, O'Callaghan declined to take it, thereby making it a gift to the diocese.

(11) Gately, Sr M J: op.cit. p 273

(12) From a short paper in the Archives of the Diocese of Little Rock entitled "General Diocesan History".

(13) Patton, Fred: op.cit. p 115

(14) This situation grew steadily worse and immediately after the Civil War ended in 1865, Fort Smith became the typical frontier town of old western movies. It took twenty years for Judge Parker and his marshalls to change the image of Fort Smith.

(15) "Fort Smith Herald", 11th March, 1851

(16) Headstone in Calvary Cemetery, Fort Smith. This date indicates that the Breens didn't stay long in Little Rock. The group had arrived there around December 20th and the Breens were in Roseville by January 15th.

(17) Martin, Amelia: op.cit

(18) "Arkansas Gazette", 11th July, 1851. This article had originally appeared in the "Fort Smith Herald" July 4th.

(19) ibid, 25th July, 1851. From "Fort Smith Herald" July 18th

(20) Data prepared by Melissa Pope Baldwin, historian of the Hendricks and Breen family.

(21) Memories of Bessie Hendricks written down by Mary Sheehan.

(22) ibid

(23) This was his stated occupation in the 1880 Census. The 1860 Census had described him as a labourer.

(24) Letter to the author from Michaele Breen Fulton, 27 Sept 1993

(25) Eliza was born on July 12th, 1837 and it is uncertain when she arrived in the United States. One source gives the year as 1853. Captain Hugh Rogers, whom she later married, was a steamboat captain. He was also Irish, having been born in County Armagh in 1812 and it would appear that he arrived in Fort Smith about five months before the Fr Hore group. However, he had lived in Pittsburg for many years, having emigrated to America with his parents when he was twelve years old.

I am indebted to Thelma Daggs Tankersley for this information. Mrs Tankersley is a granddaughter of William Dagg, and daughter of William's son James.

(26) Letter from Jerry Hendricks to the author dated June 30th, 1993

(27) My thanks to Alberta Johnson Blackburn for this, and other, information.

(28) Letter to the author from Jim Kelly, 29th September 1993

(29) Article 'Tobias Kelly' by N.J.Kelly, Fort Smith Historical Society Journal

(30) Letter to the author from Bitsy Cates, 22nd June, 1993

Chapter Eleven: Plan B

(1) This is the estimate of Kenneth Schmitz. Of the 470 people on the 'Ticonderoga', only about sixteen families stayed in Arkanasas. The size of the Texas-bound contingent is unknown, but was probably small and it is unlikely that many stayed in New Orleans. There could well have been upwards of three hundred of the group in St Louis.

(2) See Appendix 2 for details of the families.

(3) "St Louis Intelligencer". Various.

(4) Sullivan, Dr Margaret Lo Piccolo: "St Louis Ethnic Neighbourhoods 1850-1930"; Bulletin of the Missouri Historical Society XXXIII:2, January 1977. Pp64-76

(4) ibid

(5) ibid

(6) ibid

(7) According to Gately, many of them opened businesses and were numbered among the city's prominent citizens within a few years.

(8) Schmitz, Kenneth: "The Past" 1975/6

(9) ibid

(10) Adams, James Truslow & Coleman, R.V. (Eds.): "Dictionary of American History"; Vol.III, 2nd Edition – revised; Charles Scribner & Sons; New York; 1940. p451

(11) Descendant families still living in the area now spell the name Heffern

(12) See Appendix 2.

(13) Carl Mullarkey of Wexford, Iowa in an interview with the author in April 1993.

(14) ibid

(15) Zita Gavin of Wexford, Iowa told the author in an interview in her home in April 1993, later confirmed by letter, that mass was said on what is

now her farm "where our silo now stands for all the neighbors around. Water for the mass was used from our spring, just next to where mass was offered". When Mrs Gavin's cousin, Laurence Kelly, was ordained to the priesthood he used water from the same spring for his first mass at Harper's Ferry. Carl Mullarkey also states that mass was offered outdoors. He cites 'The Big Meadows' just in front of the present church as the location of Hore's first mass in the area.

(16) Letter to the author from Dolores Schmitt, 18th November, 1993
(17) The source for most of the dealings between Fr Hore and New Melleray referred to in this chapter is Schmitz's article.

Bibliography

BOOKS & PAMPHLETS:

Adams, James Truslow (Editor-in-Chief) & Coleman, R.V. (Managing Editor); "Dictionary of American History"; 2nd edition, revised; Charles Scribner & Son, New York; 1940.

Alexander, W. E.; "History of Winneshiek and Allamakee Counties, Iowa"; Iowa State Historical Society; Western Publishing Company, Sioux City, Iowa. 1882

"All Hallows Pioneer Priests in the United States"; 150th anniversary 1842-1992.

Allemakee County Heritage Book Committee: "Allemakee County, Iowa, History"; 1990

Bailey, James Henry II; "History of St Peter's Church, Richmond, Virgina"; Richmond, 1959

Bence-Jones, Mark (ed.); "Burke's Guide to Country Houses", Vol.1, Ireland; 1978

Burke's Peerage & Baronetcy, London 1921

Cantwell, Brian: "Memorials of the Dead"; Volumes 1-4; Greystones. 1980s

Carroll, Mother Austin: "Leaves from the Annals of the Sisters of Mercy"; Catholic Publication Society, New York; 1889

Church of the Immaculate Conception Diamond Jubilee booklet, Jubilee Committee, Fort Smith, Arkansas, 1974

Coleman, Terry; "Passage to America"; Penguin; 1976

Coleman, R.V. (Managing Editor) & Adams, James Truslow (Editor-in-Chief); "Dictionary of American History"; 2nd edition, revised; Charles Scribner & Son, New York; 1940.

Encyclopaedia Americana, International Edition; 1946.

Gately, Sr.M.J: "The Sisters of Mercy"; New York. 1931

Grattan-Flood, W: "History of the Diocese of Ferns"; Waterford; 1916.

Guy, Francis Joseph: "The Catholic Church in Arkansas 1541 – 1843. A dissertation"; Catholic University of America, 1932

Hancock, Ellery M.: "Past and Present of Allemakee County, Iowa" – A Record of Settlement, Organisation, Progress and Achievement; The S.J.Clarke Publishing Company, Chicago; 1913. Vol. 1

Herron, Sr.M.Eulalia,phd: "The Sisters of Mercy in the United States, 1843-1928"; MacMillan & Co, New York; 1929.

Jackson, Gordon: "The History and Archaeology of Ports"; World's Work Ltd, 1983

Kelly, Sr Mary, OP: "Catholic Immigrant Colonization Projects in the United States, 1815-1860"; U.S. Catholic Historical Society, New York, 1939

Lewis's Topographical Dictionary 1837

McGowan, Rev John, C.M: "The Irish Famine of 1847"; Sister M. Assisi (ed); Sisters of the Holy Faith, Dublin, 1967

Murphy, Hilary; "Families of Co. Wexford"; Geography Publications, Dublin; 1986.

Neal, Frank; "Sectarian Violence – The Liverpool Experience 1819-1914: An Aspect of Anglo-Irish History"; Manchester University Press; 1988.

Neill, Kenneth; "An Illustrated History of the Irish People"; Gill and MacMillan, Dublin, 1979

Niehaus, Earl F, S.M.: "The Irish in New Orleans": A History of St Patrick's parish, New Orleans 1833-1958

O'Connell, Maurice R.(ed): "The Correspondence of Daniel O'Connell"; Vol 4, 1829 -31; Irish University Press for the Irish Manuscripts Commission, 1974.

Pakenham, Thomas; "The Year of Liberty"; London, 1972

Patton, J.Fred; "History of Fort Smith, Arkansas. 1817-1992"; Fort Smith; 1992

Roche, Richard; "The Texas Connection: The Story of the Wexford Colony in Refugio"; County Wexford Heritage Committee, County Hall, Wexford, Ireland. 1989

Shea, Michael: "Maritime England"; Country Life Books in association with the English Tourist Board, London, 1981

Sisters of Mercy with Jane Ramos: "Arkansas Frontiers of Mercy"; Fort Smith; 1989

Slater's Directory, 1846.

Smyth, Hazel P.; "The B&I Line. A History of the British and Irish Steam Packet Company"; Gill and MacMillan; 1984

Thom's Directory; Dublin 1841 to 1851 inclusive

Woodham-Smith, Cecil; "The Great Hunger. Ireland 1845 – 1849". Hamish Hamilton, London; 1962

Woodmansee, Dale P; "Allamakee County, Iowa, Burial Grounds 1845-1988"; Waukon; 1989

JOURNALS AND NEWSPAPERS:

American Irish Historical Society, Journal of. Vol 9, 1910

"An Sleibhteanach", Cholaiste Chnuic Mhelleri, Co Waterford. 1902

"Arkansas Gazette". Various

"Bulletin of the Missouri Historical Society" XXXIII; 2 January, 1977

"Courier", Liverpool, 1850

"Democrat", Waukon, Iowa. 15/7/1948

"Enniscorthy Echo", Co. Wexford, Ireland. 6/9/1985

"Fort Smith Herald", Arkansas. Various

Fort Smith Historical Society Journal, 1978
"Freeman's Journal", Dublin. Various
"Herald", Dubuque, Iowa. 30/6/1935.
"Illustrated London News". Various.
"Independent", Wexford, Ireland. Various
"The Iowan – Iowa's own Magazine"; Vol. 5 No. 5; June/July 1957.
"Journal", Lansing, Iowa. Various
"Liverpool Journal", Liverpool, 1850
"Liverpool Mercury", Liverpool, 1850
"Liverpool Telegraph and Shipping Gazette", Liverpool, 1850
"Liverpool Times", Liverpool, 1850
"Lloyds Lists", London, 1850/51
"The Past", Journal of the Cumann Seanchais Ui Cinsealaigh. No. XI, 1975/6 & No. XII, 1978
"The People", Wexford, Ireland. Various
"Press Citizen", Iowa City, Iowa. 17/7/1948
"Southwest Times Record", Fort Smith, Arkansas. 26/5/1974
"St Louis Intelligencer". Various.
West Wicklow Historical Society, Journal of. Various.
Wicklow Historical Society Journal. Various.

DOCUMENTS & MANUSCRIPT RECORDS:

Census of Ireland 1841
Census Indexes 1860, for Refugio, Little Rock, Fort Smith and St Louis.
Cullen Papers, Dublin Diocesan Archives. 39/2/File VII. Letter numbers: 1,6,25,28,30,31,36,39,43,44,54,59.
Customs Entry Bills, Port of Liverpool, William Brown Library, Liverpool
Fitzwilliam Papers, National Library of Ireland. Various
Hendrick(s)/Breen Papers. Various letters and recorded reminicences relating to the history of the family. Particularly the genealogy prepared by Melissa Baldwin.
Outrage Reports, National Archives (Ireland). 1850. 32/105
Parliamentary Papers: Trade Navigation; 1852/3 (205);
Vol.xcviii: 335
Passenger Lists of the 'Ticonderoga', 'Loodianah' and 'Chasca'
Various correspondence referred to in the NOTES.

List of Subscribers

Buddy Hendricks, Barling, Arkansas
Mary Breen Culp, Muldrow, Oklahoma
James B. Kelly, Houston, Texas
Leota Kelly Hopkins, Cleburne, Texas
Franklin F. Kelly, Sinton , Texas
Owen O'Neill, Tipperary
Patricia Bolger Hieb, Ponsford, Minnesota
Inez Daggs Hobbs, Hartford, Arkansas
Bertie Daggs O'Brien, Hartford, Arkansas
Zita Gavin, Harper's Ferry, Iowa
Gwen Johnson, Abilene, Kansas
Cheri Castillow, Little Rock, Arkansas
Betsy Hendricks Walters, Springfield, Missouri
Rev Joseph Correnti, Little Rock, Arkansas
Julia Mae Campbell, Little Rock, Arkansas
Alberta Johnson Blackburn, Ada, Kansas
Julie Ann Stec, Fort Smith, Arkansas
Marlene E. Payne, Vestal, New York
Betty Schoen, Pocola, Oklahoma
Eddie Alan McInnes, Sand Springs, Oklahoma
David R. McInnes, Humble, Texas
Karen A. Brown, Midwest City, Oklahoma
Thelma (Daggs) Tankersley, Midwest City, Oklahoma
Michaele Breen Fulton, Sherwood, Arkansas
Peggy Stevenson, Little Rock, Arkansas
Melissa Baldwin, Jonesboro, Arkansas
Leroy T. Pickle, Hartford, Arkansas

Mrs. William Dudley, Lynchburg, Virginia
Mary Lynn Lawler, Kansas City, Missouri
Irene Pickle Pitchford, Greenwood, Arkansas
Flora Daggs Pickle, Fort Smith, Arkansas
Rhonda Pitchford Kralicek, Little Rock, Arkansas
Nancy Pitchford Mixon, Fort Smith, Arkansas
Alisia Pitchford Scallions, Fort Smith, Arkansas
Mr. & Mrs. J. L. Pickle, Fort Smith, Arkansas
Mr. & Mrs. K. C. Pickle, Wilmington, Carolina
Mrs Ralph (Cullen) Bennett, Fort Smith, Arkansas
Dolores M. Schmitt, Madison, Wisconsin
Debi Woodward, Fort Smith, Arkansas
Lt C. (Retd.) M. K. Hopkins, Brandon, Florida
Bodie Hatcher, Fort Smith, Arkansas
Sally Hendricks Marovich, Evergreen, Colorado
Mary Jeanne Bradney Black, Fort Smith, Arkansas
Carl & Ramona Mullarkey, Lansing, Iowa
Patty Manning, Lansing, Iowa
Regina Manning, Lansing, Iowa
John O'Neill, Harper's Ferry, Iowa
Dennis & Ellen Manning, Lansing, Iowa

Alice Conway, Harper's Ferry, Iowa
Clifton Daggs, Fort Smith, Arkansas
Laura Hendricks Elwood, Fort Smith, Arkansas
Mark & Marsha (Manning) Kruse, Lansing
Sharon Truong, Barling, Arkansas
Margaret Breen Thompson, Oklahoma City
Robie Memorial Library, Waukon, Iowa
Angela Hendricks Upchurch, Fort Smith, Arkansas
Patrick & Mary Sharon Curran, Lansing, Iowa
Patricia Breen Harder, Phoenix, Arizona
Mrs Joseph (Irene) Deeney, Waukon, Iowa
Mr & Mrs Walter Keenan, Waukon, Iowa
Donald Pettigrew, Huntsville, Alabama
Sr Rebecca Hendricks, Fort Smith, Arkansas
Janie Hendricks Freeze, Fort Smith, Arkansas
Erma Bailey, Fort Smith, Arkansas
James J. Breen, Jr., C harleston, Arkansas

Dr. Stephen Regan, Elkader, Iowa
Randolph Teague, Arlington, Texas
Shirley Teague, Fort Smith, Arkansas
Francis & Leonette Kernan, Lansing, Iowa
Mary Jo (Gavin) Mohn, Lansing, Iowa
Paudge Brennan, Carnew, Co Wicklow
State Historical Society of Iowa, Iowa City
Rebecca Ann Thompson, (Breen family), Oklahoma City
Barbara Ann Jackson, (Breen family), Oklahoma City
Glenn Ray Thompson, (Breen family), Katy, Texas
Nancy Jean Kyle, (Breen family), Oklahoma City
Peggy (Margaret) Mailer, Fort Smith, Arkansas
Amelia Whitaker Martin, Fort Smith, Arkansas
Mary Steffen, Lansing, Iowa
Shirley Breen Gammill Sack, Oklahoma City